The Making of an Advertising Campaign

Jaye S. Niefeld
Bozell, Jacobs, Kenyon & Eckhardt, Inc.

Prentice Hall, Englewood Cliffs, New Jersey 07632

Library of Congress Cataloging-in-Publication Data
Niefeld, Jaye Sutter.
  The making of an advertising campaign.
  1. Advertising campaigns. I. Title.
HF5827.N75 1989   659.1   88-31713
ISBN 0-13-546193-6

Editorial/production supervision and
  interior design: **Eleanor Ode Walter**
Cover design: **Ben Santora**
Manufacturing buyers: **Margaret Rizzi, Laura Crossland**
Page layout: **Karen Noferi**

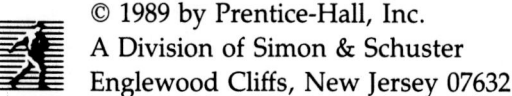

© 1989 by Prentice-Hall, Inc.
A Division of Simon & Schuster
Englewood Cliffs, New Jersey 07632

All rights reserved. No part of this book may be
reproduced, in any form or by any means,
without permission in writing from the publisher.

Printed in the United States of America
10 9 8 7 6 5 4 3 2 1

ISBN 0-13-546193-6

Prentice-Hall International (UK) Limited, *London*
Prentice-Hall of Australia Pty. Limited, *Sydney*
Prentice-Hall Canada Inc., *Toronto*
Prentice-Hall Hispanoamericana, S.A., *Mexico*
Prentice-Hall of India Private Limited, *New Delhi*
Prentice-Hall of Japan, Inc., *Tokyo*
Simon & Schuster Asia Pte. Ltd., *Singapore*
Editora Prentice-Hall do Brasil, Ltda., *Rio de Janeiro*

To Charles D. Peebler, Jr., a remarkable executive who transformed an obscure, Omaha-based advertising agency into one of the top dozen agencies in the world. He has been both colleague and friend for almost twenty years.

Contents

	Preface	vii
Chapter 1	Introduction	1
Chapter 2	Planning the Campaign	5
Chapter 3	The Target Groups	31
Chapter 4	The Media Plan	45
Chapter 5	Public Relations	51
Chapter 6	The Creative Work	63
Chapter 7	Merchandising	91
Chapter 8	Conclusion	101

Preface

The question might well be asked, "Why has it taken so long to publish a book on the making of an advertising campaign?" After all, thousands of campaigns are prepared every year, and heaven knows that, for a student interested in a career in advertising or for someone simply interested in the general subject, it is hard to conceive of a book that would be more useful than one that describes how an advertising agency goes about the task of creating a campaign.

The most basic impediment to a book on this subject is simple: Almost all advertising campaigns are the property of the advertisers for whom the campaigns are prepared, and advertisers are reluctant to surrender a competitive edge. "Does Macy's tell Gimbel's?" is a question almost invariably answered in the negative.

There are other factors, though. For instance, relatively few campaigns are complete unto themselves. Except for those that introduce new products, most are based on experience and information gathered at some earlier time. And more often than might be readily admitted, the preparatory work is based on subjective judgment rather than on hard (or, for that matter, soft) data.

In addition, although almost all advertising agencies are fully aware of systematic procedures for planning and executing an advertising campaign, they frequently find it impractical, unprofitable or too time-consuming to follow such procedures. Then there is a small group of agencies that prefer to rely on creative inspiration rather than on any methodical preparatory process.

There are also times when it is the advertiser who insists on short-circuiting the systematic procedure. The client may opt to do this to save time or money or both. Unfortunately, short-circuiting often results in a less-than-successful effort. One rather frustrated lament in the trade is, We didn't have the time (or money) to do it right the first time, but somehow we found enough to do it over again. But do not let this comment confuse the realities of the situation. The lack of adequate time is endemic to our business. Competition in the marketplace seems to create the ulcer-generating time pressures that advertising people learn to live with. And it is unlikely that any client or agency will ever completely eliminate those pressures.

It was only the convergence of certain competitive factors that persuaded Bozell, Jacobs, Kenyon & Eckhardt to develop the campaign described in this volume. Chapter 1 discusses the genesis of the campaign that led to this book.

ACKNOWLEDGMENTS

Every advertising campaign is the result of the combined efforts of many people. This one is no exception. Although I had overall responsibility for the project and specific responsibility for several elements of it, indispensable contributions were made by various members of the Bozell, Jacobs, Kenyon & Eckhardt staff.

Particular thanks for the creative work go to John LaPick and his group in the agency's Los Angeles office and to John Lindsey in our Chicago office, who did much to prepare the graphic material for publication. Les Gibson and his people in the agency's Dallas office executed the leave-behind piece and created, with the generous cooperation of the Neiman Marcus organization, the merchandising materials. The market research was supervised by Dr. Renee Fraser, and the media approach was prepared by James Spero, both of our Los Angeles office. The section on public relations was originally prepared by Robert Bagar of our New York office. A special word of thanks to the team that made the first formal presentation of the campaign in the Great Hall of the People in Beijing, China. In addition to me, the presenters were David A. Bell, John LaPick, and Murray L. Smith.

On a very personal level, I want to express my gratitude to Terry Gruggen of the agency's Minneapolis office for his beyond-the-call-of-duty dedication to this project in a dozen different and essential ways and to Diane Bonner of the Chicago office for helping to guide the project through its various phases. Thanks also to Larry Dobrow, Bozell's director of corporate communications, who had the felicitous notion that our Beijing presentation would make a useful textbook, and to Whitney Blake of Prentice Hall who agreed with him. Also at Prentice Hall, I am indebted to Eleanor Walter of the Editorial-Production Department.

There is one "outsider" who should be mentioned. Dr. Harry L. Davis, deputy dean of the University of Chicago's Graduate School of Business, described to me his experience teaching Chinese students in Beijing about Western economic systems. Based on his experience, several elements were included in the presentation in Beijing that made the entire project far more meaningful to the audience than would otherwise have been the case.

A final note in this preface: The reader will encounter several interoffice memos in this book. They are included to give the reader the flavor of the process we went through. Most are the actual memos sent at various phases of the campaign's development. Some of the memos, however, are written paraphrases of what were actually conversations—held mostly between the author and various individuals responsible for specific sections of the project.

Chapter 1

Introduction

The assignment was unique by any standards—a once-in-a-lifetime opportunity. *SOUTH* magazine was sponsoring an advertising conference in Beijing. There were two basic objectives: (1) to explain to the West the Chinese manner of conducting business and (2) to explain our Western ways of conducting business to China and other Third World countries. Bozell, Jacobs, Kenyon & Eckhardt was invited to participate in the conference by preparing a prototypical example of how an American advertising agency would approach the following subject:

> The presentation of an advertising campaign illustrating how an image campaign for China in the West would in turn have beneficial effects on all products made in China.

This meant demonstrating the procedure an American advertising agency would normally follow in approaching an assignment of this type—complete with market research, marketing and creative strategies, a full set of creative materials, media planning, merchandising, public relations, and, finally, a presentation to those attending the conference that would be worthy of the campaign.

The cost of preparing this kind of advertising program is extremely high, and few agencies would normally be willing to spend the necessary money. Our agency was prepared to make this very considerable investment because our chief executive officer, Charles Peebler, wanted to achieve a higher profile for the agency's relatively small international division.

Therefore, the agency's willingness to participate in the conference with an extraordinary effort was a planned strategy rather than an impulsive decision.

Memorandum

Bozell, Jacobs, Kenyon & Eckhardt, Inc.
Advertising

MEMO TO: Jaye S. Niefeld

FROM: Charles D. Peebler, Jr.

RE: Advertising Conference

There is going to be an Advertising Conference in June in Beijing, China and we've been asked by our old friend, Jim Fleury, to participate in the program.

Because the audience will consist of 1,500 representatives of foreign governments and multi-national companies, I think this Conference may be the best opportunity we'll have in some time to increase the visibility of our International Division in Asia.

Other U.S. agencies will also be presenting, but I want our presentation to dominate the Conference.

I would like you to direct this project and would appreciate hearing from you about how you plan to proceed.

All the best,

Memorandum

Bozell, Jacobs, Kenyon & Eckhardt, Inc.
Advertising

MEMO TO: Charles D. Peebler, Jr.

FROM: Jaye S. Niefeld

RE: Beijing Advertising Conference

After receiving your memo on the Beijing Advertising Conference, I talked with Murray Smith. He and I are going to Hong Kong next week to confer with Jim Fleury who, as you know, is managing the Conference. We want to find out what Fleury would like us to prepare for the program.

My thought is that we should produce a complete and quite elaborate presentation in order to accomplish your objectives of heightening awareness of and respect for our International Division.

That incidentally means that you ought to be thinking about a pretty substantial budget. I'll give you my thought on money after we decide what it is that we'll present.

If we do an elaborate presentation, I'm going to ask Jim to give us a very favorable time on the program -- not, for example, the afternoon of the last day of the Conference. My choice of a time slot would be some time the second day of the five-day Conference.

Cordially,

Charles D. Peebler, Jr. was chief executive officer of Bozell, Jacobs, Kenyon & Eckhardt; Jaye Niefeld was executive vice president; and Murray Smith was president of the agency's international division.

Memorandum

Bozell, Jacobs, Kenyon & Eckhardt, Inc.
Advertising

MEMO TO: Terry Gruggen

FROM: Jaye S. Niefeld

RE: Beijing Conference

As I mentioned in our telephone conversation this morning, I'm asking you to help coordinate the Beijing Advertising Conference presentation. As of now, these are my thoughts on who's to do what:

1. Although we're not expecting any specific new clients as a direct result of this presentation, I feel that the agency's office that is most likely to benefit from the Conference is Los Angeles. Therefore, I'm going to clear with Cy Schneider that that office do most of the work -- creative, media and research.

2. Public relations is best handled out of our New York office, if for no other reason that they have the largest staff. The P.R. departments in our other offices would find it very difficult to make time for this project.

3. Since the presentation will be unusually complete, I want to prepare a leave-behind piece which will contain verbatim the text of the presentation, as well as all of the creative material. Les Gibson's group in Dallas has the most experience of anyone in the agency in this area, so use him.

4. Everyone working on this project, including yourself, will be having to continue with regular duties in addition to the work on the Conference. Meeting a June deadline, therefore, will not be easy. Use my assistant, Diane Bonner, whenever you feel she can be of help in shepherding the assignments through.

I'd like progress reports every week for the foreseeable future.

Cordially,

Chapter 2

Planning the Campaign

SETTING THE CAMPAIGN OBJECTIVES

The purpose of this project was to demonstrate how a contemporary advertising agency creates an advertising campaign. One of our problems was communicating this process to a group of people who were not familiar with certain aspects of American society.

All of the above meant that the presentation would have to explain several cultural differences before the audience was able to grasp what we were trying to do. Some Asian countries have quite different attitudes about what is socially acceptable and what is risqué or even obscene. We did not want to step over that attitudinal line, so it was clear that we would have to account for certain disparities in our respective cultures.

Therefore, our general objectives were (1) to demonstrate the process of creating an advertising campaign and (2) to have our audience understand that process, taking into account obvious cultural differences. Our specific objective was to demonstrate that an image advertising campaign for China would have a beneficial effect on the sale of Chinese products in the West. After some reflection, we decided that we should concentrate on a single product—silk—rather than try to show the effect of image advertising on all Chinese products. Our choice of product will become clear in the discussion of the results of our research findings.

Memorandum

Bozell, Jacobs, Kenyon & Eckhardt, Inc.
Advertising

MEMO TO: Charles D. Peebler, Jr.

FROM: Jaye S. Niefeld

RE: Beijing Conference

Murray Smith and I had a meeting with Jim Fleury in Hong Kong and decided on the following:

1. The subject we are to discuss on the Conference program is "The presentation of an advertising campaign illustrating how an image campaign for China in the West would in turn have beneficial effects on all products made in China."

   Originally the subject read "The presentation of a fictional advertising campaign..." but I feel that the case history should be "real" not "fictional." We also agreed that we should not use the generic "Chinese products" but instead should focus on one specific product. After some discussion, we agreed that Chinese silk would be the best product to use.

2. Our original time on the program was for 20 minutes on the second day of the Conference. When I explained that we planned to prepare an unusually complete presentation, including fairly finished television and print advertising, Jim agreed to give us the 90 minutes we asked for.

   We're also presenting on the second day of the Conference but in the afternoon unfortunately.

Subsequent to that meeting, Murray and I held a meeting in the Hong Kong office with Mike Anderson, Joe Wang, and Joseph Tong (of China-Link). The two Chinese were particularly concerned that our presentation be done with full sensitivity to the cultural differences between Chinese and Americans.

I've agreed to submit our recommendations -- particularly the creative work -- to make sure we have no offensive elements, although I explained to Joe and Joseph that this campaign is one that would run in the U.S., not China.

Therefore, if we did have material that jarred the Chinese, we'd simply have to explain to the audience that Americans would not take offense at this work.

In fact, my inclination now is to have a short section at the beginning of our presentation that would familiarize the audience with aspects of U.S. advertising (particularly the tone of our advertising) that differ from the Asian.

At a meeting the next day with Messrs. Anderson, Smith, Tong, and Wang, I presented an outline for the presentation. With an additional suggestion or two, the outline was agreed upon.

As soon as I've worked up a little more detail, I'll send you a copy.

Cordially,

WHAT GOES INTO A CAMPAIGN?

There are four essential steps in the making of an advertising campaign:

1. Defining the target group
2. Determining the appeal or creative strategy that will be most effective with the target group
3. Executing the creative strategy in the most arresting and appealing fashion
4. Selecting the most effective and cost-efficient media to reach the target group

Everything else that an agency does is an extension, execution, embellishment, or evaluation of this process.

Although the project would require a considerable amount of research, the procedure was no different from the preparatory work that goes into most other types of campaigns. We depend on research to help manage risk, help increase advertising productivity, develop communication strategies, and teach us more about how advertising works in conjunction with other marketing activities (e.g., sales promotion). More specifically, we need answers to the following questions:

1. Target markets: Who are the product's prime prospects?
2. The competitive frame: Where will sales increases come from?
3. Leverage: What is the advertising appeal—and the support for that appeal—that will motivate the product's prime prospects?

THE RESULT OF THE RESEARCH

The product strategy that emerges from the answers to these questions provides us with both the guidelines for creative development and the means for evaluating the advertising. Traditionally, the information fits into the following total communication plan:

1. Market profile
2. Problems and opportunities
3. Objectives
4. Strategy development
5. The communication plan
6. The operating plan
7. Evaluation and refinement

TARGET-GROUP DESCRIPTION

A target-group description should be one that enables the advertiser to focus both creative and media strategies on groups that are relatively homogeneous. Targets should therefore be based on a relevant factor such as age, psychological makeup, income, or lifestyle.

Strategically, the definition of the target group is undoubtedly the single most important step in the advertising process. Research defines the parameters

Chap. 2 / Planning the Campaign

The Research Design

Memorandum

Bozell, Jacobs, Kenyon & Eckhardt, Inc.
Advertising

MEMO TO: Murray Smith

FROM: Jaye Niefeld

RE: China Presentation

Attached is a description of the presentation for Jim Fleury and a copy for you. I hope this suffices for the publicity material Jim is preparing. We obviously won't have a completed script for some time -- not until after we've completed the creative materials and research, so I guess this will have to do for now.

Michael was able to confirm meetings with China-Link for April 7 and a PRC representative in Beijing for April 9. Prior to that time (about March 25), I'll have gone to L.A. and gotten prototype commercials and ads which we can submit to the Chinese to make sure we're not violating some legal or cultural taboo.

Naturally, I'll keep you posted.

Cordially,

THIRD WORLD ADVERTISING CONGRESS - BEIJING

Assignment:

"Presentation of an advertising campaign illustrating how an image campaign for China in the West would in turn have beneficial effects on all products made in China."

The Presentation:

It is our intention to use this case history to illustrate how a major advertising agency in the United States approachs an important advertising assignment. It will be, in other words, a kind of textbook example, using this problem as the subject.

I. Welcome and discussion of the assignment and its objectives. The image campaign for China will be actual, not fictional. And rather than show the effects on "all products made in China," we have chosen one specific product -- silk -- and will demonstrate how the image campaign helps sell this specific product in the United States.

II. As background for the audience, we will explain U.S. customer types and selling practices, which specifically involve:

A. Designers
B. Apparel manufacturers
C. Retailers and retailers' buyers
D. Customers

III. Again, as background for the audience, we will explain U.S. conceptions and misconceptions about China. This material will be based on original research, conducted specifically for this assignment.

IV. Strategies

A. The strategy for the Chinese image campaign in the U.S. will depend upon the results of the market research we conduct, but some points to remember are:

... China has a 5,000 year tradition of craftsmanship dedicated to the creating of products known for their beauty and quality. This tradition is seen dramatically in such products as Chinese silk, ivory, porcelain, jade, sculpture, and rugs.

B. The strategy for the Chinese silk campaign will also be based on research results, but keep in mind:

   ...   Today, as it has been for five millenia, silk is treasured as a unique, beautiful, and luxurious fabric -- used in the most prestigious products. Consumers who wish the very best prefer pure Chinese silk, which is why more of the rare textile comes from China that from all of the thirty-four other silk-producing countries combined.

C. The target groups for these campaigns are:

   1. Designers.
   2. Apparel manufacturers.
   3. Retailers and retailers' buyers.
   4. Because of silk's uniqueness and expensiveness, our campaign is directed specifically to these customer groups (according to the VALS typology):

      ...Achievers
      ...The Societally Conscious

V. Tactics

A. Advertising campaigns for each target group

   This section will contain specific advertising campaigns for each of the four target groups, including television commercials where appropriate and print media advertising. The material will include an image campaign, as well as advertising for Chinese silk.

B. Point-of-sale materials

   This section will contain examples of some point-of-sale materials as part of a successful support program for Chinese silk. It will also demonstrate how an upscale American department store would promote Chinese silk.

C. Media plans for each target group, as well as an international plan, will be presented recognizing, however, the need to keep hard-currency advertising budgets to a sensible level.

D. Plans for a public relations program which could supplement an advertising program will also be presented.

VI. Creative Research

   The advertising materials will be thoroughly researched to make sure they convey the messages that were spelled out in the strategies.

VII. Conclusion

   This section will comprise concluding remarks, a brief reprise of the creative work, and an invitation to the audience to accept a leave-behind binder that includes all of the material covered in the presentation.

Memorandum

Bozell, Jacobs, Kenyon & Eckhardt, Inc.
Advertising

MEMO TO: Renee Fraser

FROM: Jaye S. Niefeld

RE: Research on Chinese Silk

I'm also very excited about the Beijing challenge. As we discussed this morning, the research is a critical first step in the project. Because everything else we do depends on the research, it is important that it be well done and promptly. Your estimate of nine weeks for completion is O.K. That puts us at April 7, but any time you can pick up would be most welcome.

I've listed below the areas I think the research should cover:

1. How familiar are Americans with China and Chinese products? How does that compare with our familiarity with other Asian or Middle Eastern countries?

2. What reputation do Chinese products have in this country? How does that reputation compare with products of other countries?

3. Which products do Americans expect from China and how interested are Americans in buying those products?

4. No one has asked for it, but why not also see what we can learn about the potential for American tourism to China? Tourism may turn out to have far more potential than is true of any product.

Simmons and VALS have already given us the information we need on target groups. ACHIEVERS and the SOCIETALLY CONSCIOUS are definitely the segments so please conduct the research among those two groups. Although BELONGERS are below average in per capita consumption, they are such a large proportion of the population, I'd include them too.

Renee Fraser was director of strategic planning for the agency's Los Angeles office.

Finally, a technical point. As you know, Americans are usually very weak in geography. I think they may have a tough time differentiating between "The People's Republic of China" and Taiwan and Hong Kong. I'd like you to consider referring to the P.R.C. as "Mainland China."

When you have developed a questionnaire, please let me know.

Best wishes,

of the group and then refines and interprets the information. The end result is a profile of the "typical" target user—a single person. The agency's creative writers and art directors concentrate their creative efforts on this single, prototypical consumer. Media specialists determine how best to reach the target consumer in the most effective, cost-efficient manner.

SYNDICATED RESEARCH SERVICES

Syndicated research services provide information on product usage by various types of consumers. Most frequently, this information is demographic. For example, although 77.1 percent of adults drink coffee, only 27.5 percent are heavy users of the brew. Unfortunately, although these data are convenient, they are not always useful. For example, heavy users of many food products often are described as "women 18 to 49 years of age." This description is an illusory one, not a valid target-group description: Women of 18 have little or nothing in common with women of 49. The former are likely still to be in high school, while the latter can easily be grandmothers! Indeed, it is probable that the *only* thing they have in common is their gender. It is hard to visualize a creative appeal that would have equal relevance to 18-year-olds and 49-year-olds. Even media selection would be quite different for the diverse ages within this category.

RELATING THE RESEARCH STUDY TO OUR CHINA PROJECT

As previously discussed, the subject of our project was "The presentation of an advertising campaign, illustrating how an image campaign for China in the West would in turn have beneficial effects on all products made in China." Therefore, the first thing we needed to know was whether our premise was a valid one. That is, would an image campaign in the West really help China sell its products here? If Americans who are *familiar* with China are more inclined to purchase Chinese products than people who are *not* familiar with China, the premise would be justified.

Conversely, if people unfamiliar with China were just as likely—or even more likely—to purchase Chinese products, then the basic idea of the project would have to be considered invalid. Appropriate market research would help us resolve this issue.

Assuming that the basic premise held up, the research study could also give us some valuable clues concerning (1) which Chinese products would be most easily sold in this country, (2) the proper target group, and (3) the creative strategy that would be most effective with that group. Our study was specifically aimed at determining

- How familiar Americans are with China and its products
- What reputation the products have among various segments of the American public
- What products Americans expect from China
- How interested Americans are in buying Chinese products
- How American perceptions of Chinese products differ from perceptions of products of other countries of the Orient and the Middle East

Additionally, because we thought the Chinese tourism industry might be interested in Americans' attitudes on travel to China, we also included a question on how likely Americans were to consider visiting that country.

The data were collected in telephone interviews with a national sample of U.S. adults. A total of 297 interviews were conducted. Half of the interviews were with men and half with women. Approximately 100 interviews came from each of three key consumer segments: achievers, the societally conscious, and belongers.

These segments are part of a consumer typology named VALS (for Values and Lifestyles), which was developed by SRI International, a research organization. There is a more detailed discussion of the VALS typology in Chapter 3.

Note: Normally, a sample of 1,500 or more would be needed to represent reliably the population of the United States. National political polls and television audience measurements usually use samples of approximately that size. Such samples are looking for results that are extremely precise—often within a percentage point or less. In political races a couple of percentage points frequently are the difference between winner and loser. In television programming, a percentage point or two may determine whether a show will live or die or how much a network may charge for commercial time on that show.

In this case, however, a high degree of reliability was not essential because we were demonstrating the *process* rather than the precision of the findings. Confidence levels of 90 percent are usually considered sufficient for most marketing purposes, but the cost to achieve the last 5 to 10 percent accuracy can be extremely high.

QUALITATIVE VERSUS QUANTITATIVE RESEARCH

There are various types of consumer research. Qualitative and quantitative research are two of the types. Qualitative research usually provides the user with the *feeling* of really understanding what is going on in the consumer's mind. Respondents are asked to speak freely about a particular product. They are encouraged to express their opinions about various subjects, such as alternative brands. However, because each analyst interprets the data subjectively, the findings can be inaccurately weighted toward ideas that either support favored hypotheses or are highly unusual, unexpected, or entertaining.

Quantitative research is different. It *measures* the respondent's attitude, frequently toward some aspect of a product. Consumers are given the opportunity to express their agreement or disagreement only with the subjects the researcher has seen as important. This sounds very straightforward, but it is not. Quantitative research questions are usually worded in a way that allows the respondent to register "standing attitudes," that is, attitudes that are stored in that person's memory. The results are generally accepted as a valid indication of what consumers will do and why, even though, in setting up the questionnaire, the researcher may have inadvertently omitted questions that dealt with aspects of critical importance.

There is much about human behavior that suggests that the relationship between attitudes and behavior is much more complex than can be ascertained through quantitative research. For example, an overweight person might strongly believe that eating sweets is bad for him or her and express that standing attitude when probed by researchers, yet still say yes when the waiter asks if he or she would like dessert.

It becomes apparent that the ready acceptance of standing attitudes expressed in quantitative research may be inappropriate to many kinds of projects. Instead, the attitudes that are evoked into consciousness at the *time of choice* are frequently more critical. For example, the overweight person discussed above certainly "knows" the undesirable consequences of having dessert. This

Memorandum

Bozell, Jacobs, Kenyon & Eckhardt, Inc.
Advertising

MEMO TO: Jaye S. Niefeld

FROM: Renee Fraser

RE: Chinese Silk Research

We're getting ready to field the research on U.S. attitudes toward China and Chinese silk. Enclosed is a copy of the final questionnaire, which I think covers all of the objectives and the suggestions outlined in your last memo.

I've decided to limit the number of respondents to 300. After all, we're simply trying to illustrate the process we use, and that doesn't require the 90% to 95% level of confidence in the responses that we would normally strive for.

We're conducting mall intercepts in Los Angeles and Chicago: half of the respondents will be men, half women; and we'll interview ACHIEVERS, the SOCIETALLY CONSCIOUS, and BELONGERS.

It looks as though we'll need every day of the nine weeks to complete the study, but if we can save a little time, we'll certainly do it.

One encouraging note: We will definitely stay within the budget you've set for the research.

All the best,

Renee Fraser

information is stored in his or her long-term memory. However, it may not influence that person's behavior at the moment of choice.

Normally, our research for this project would include certain qualitative sections, but in this case we opted for a study that was essentially quantitative in nature. We felt that more sophisticated techniques (e.g., qualitative or "choice-time" thoughts) were not necessary to demonstrate the process and might well be beyond the level of sophistication of a large segment of the audience.

THE FINDINGS

How Familiar Are Americans with China and Its Products?

Half of the people in the United States are admittedly unfamiliar with China and Chinese products. But there are other countries with which even more American consumers are unfamiliar—Thailand, the Caribbean islands, Singapore, India, and Australia.

Question: For each country, please tell me how familiar you are with the country and the products that country manufactures.

TABLE 2-1

COUNTRY/REGION	PERCENT UNFAMILIAR (BASE: 297)
Caribbean	72
Thailand	71
Singapore	69
India	65
Australia	58
Mainland China	50
Korea	23
Mexico	23
Taiwan	20
Europe	19
Hong Kong	19
Japan	5

Three VALS consumer types were included in the sample of respondents: Achievers, the Societally Conscious, and Belongers. The last type was included because they are the most numerous type, not necessarily because they are the best prospects for the purchase of clothing.

As can be seen in Table 2-2, Belongers claim to be somewhat more familiar with China and Chinese products than is the case with the two other VALS types.

TABLE 2-2

FAMILIARITY	PERCENT OF		
	Belongers	Achievers	Societally Conscious
Very familiar	4	3	4
Somewhat familiar	52	43	45
Not at all familiar	44	54	51

TABLE 2-3

COUNTRY: CAPITAL CITY	PERCENT WHO DID NOT KNOW CAPITAL OF COUNTRY (BASE: 297)
China: Beijing	44
Korea: Seoul	42
Japan: Tokyo	34

A further demonstration of the widespread lack of familiarity with China is found in the deficiency of Americans' basic knowledge about the country. Almost half (44 percent) of our sample could not identify Beijing as the capital of China. This compares with about a third who could not correctly identify the capital of Japan.

What Reputation Do Chinese Products Have Among Various Segments of the American Public?

Chinese products are generally not highly regarded by Americans. Only two of a series of nine attributes were regarded in a positive light by at least 20 percent of the respondents, as Table 2-4 indicates.

Question: Now I would like you to rate Mainland China on several characteristics pertaining to the quality of its products.

TABLE 2-4

CHARACTERISTIC	PERCENT WHO COMPLETELY AGREE (BASE: 297)
Uses "Old World" techniques in creating its products	27
Products available in United States at low prices	20
High level of craftsmanship	14
Wide variety of products easily available in the United States	13
Products sold in United States are good value	12
High standards of quality	9
Produces innovative products	6
Designs products reflecting contemporary American tastes	6
Produces products right for Americans	4

The validity of our project was based on determining whether familiarity with China and its products led to a higher regard for Chinese products. If it did, then an advertising campaign informing people about China would result in more favorable opinions about Chinese products. If familiarity did not lead to more favorable attitudes, there was nothing to be gained by image advertising designed to create that familiarity. As can be seen from Table 2-5, those familiar with China are significantly more inclined to rate Chinese products in a favorable light. The only exceptions are the responses to the characteristics "Uses 'Old World' techniques" and "Designs products reflecting contemporary American tastes."

TABLE 2-5

	PERCENT AGREEING COMPLETELY	
CHARACTERISTIC	Familiar with China (Base: 149)	Not Familiar with China (Base: 148)
Uses "Old World" techniques	27	28
Available at low prices	26	14
High level of craftsmanship	20	7
Products sold in United States are good value	17	7
Wide variety of products, easily available in the United States	17	8
High standard of quality	15	4
Produces innovative products	9	3
Produces products right for Americans	6	3
Designs products reflecting contemporary American tastes	6	5

What Products Do Americans Expect from China?

The results of our next question show that Americans associate porcelain, silk, clothing, and handcrafted jewelry with China. Agricultural and scientific equipment, along with consumer electronics, are much less known as products of China.

Question: When you think of products produced in Mainland China, which of the following products do you associate with that country?

TABLE 2-6

PRODUCT	PERCENT OF RESPONDENTS ASSOCIATING PRODUCTS WITH CHINA (BASE: 297)
Porcelain	76
Silk	75
Clothing	66
Handcrafted jewelry	50
Furniture	28
Consumer electronics (TV, VCR)	19
Scientific equipment	14
Agricultural equipment	11

Clearly, the American public expects China to market its traditional products—porcelain, silk, clothing—rather than technical or scientific products. China may be interested in selling the latter types of products, but Americans are not sure about their quality.

How Interested Are Americans in Purchasing Products of China?

Most American consumers (almost six out of ten) are willing to consider buying Chinese products, but their lack of knowledge about Chinese products and workmanship stand in the way of buying those products.

Question: How likely would you be to consider purchasing a product of Mainland China?

TABLE 2-7

LIKELIHOOD	PERCENT OF RESPONDENTS WILLING TO CONSIDER PURCHASING A PRODUCT OF CHINA (BASE: 297)
Very likely to consider buying	7
Somewhat likely to consider buying	50
Not very likely to consider buying	31
Not at all likely to consider buying	11

The Societally Conscious show the greatest willingness to consider buying Chinese products. From the point of view of geographic location of consumers, those living in the western part of the United States are generally the most interested in buying products made in China.

TABLE 2-8

LIKELIHOOD	PERCENT OF RESPONDENTS WILLING TO CONSIDER PURCHASING A PRODUCT OF CHINA (BASE: 297)
Very or somewhat likely to purchase:	
Total respondents	57
Societally Conscious	62
Western region of the United States	71

Among those familiar with China, two out of three are at least somewhat interested in buying Chinese products. Among those unfamiliar, the figure is less than half.

TABLE 2-9

CONSIDER PURCHASING	FAMILIARITY WITH CHINA	
	Percent of Those Familiar (Base: 149)	Percent of Those Not Familiar (Base: 148)
Very likely to consider	9 ⎫ 68	4 ⎫ 45
Somewhat likely to consider	59 ⎭	41 ⎭
Not very likely to consider	23	40
Not at all likely to consider	8	14

Our respondents expressed a preference for American products at the same time they confirmed a lack of familiarity with Chinese products. Interestingly, the reasons they gave for *not* being likely to consider purchasing products from China had little to do with the fact that China is a Communist country. See Table 2-10.

The fact that the Japanese have done so well in the United States shows that other countries can sell their goods in the United States if they design products to appeal to Americans and then advertise those products to create familiarity.

TABLE 2-10

REASONS	PERCENT OF RESPONDENTS
Only buy American products	23
Unfamiliar with Chinese products	21
Chinese quality not as good as U.S.	18
Do not need Chinese products	13
Chinese products not available	7
Buy American to keep Americans working	6
Do not support Communist country	3
Prices too high	2

How Do Perceptions of Products of China Differ from Perceptions of Products from Other Countries of the Orient and the Middle East?

A point of interest to us was whether people viewed Chinese products differently from products of comparable nations. The research shows that China's reputation for using "Old World" techniques in creating its products is its major strength. The same attribute is seen as characteristic of India. By way of contrast, the United States, Japan, and Korea were far less likely to be viewed in those terms.

Question: I would like you to rate China, Japan, Korea, India, and the United States on several characteristics pertaining to the quality of their products.

TABLE 2-11

CHARACTERISTIC (BASE:)	China (297)	Japan (297)	Korea (297)	India (297)	U.S. (297)
Uses "Old World" techniques	27	5	9	31	8
Products available in United States at low prices	20	34	34	10	14
High level of craftsmanship	14	59	8	9	29
Wide variety of products easily available in United States	13	76	25	6	89
Products are a good value	12	45	16	7	32
High standards of quality	9	42	5	3	30
Innovative products	6	55	4	1	57
Products reflect contemporary American tastes	6	55	14	2	78
Products right for Americans	4	52	11	2	69
Average	12%	47%	14%	8%	45%
Average without "Old World"	11%	52%	15%	5%	50%

It is clear from Table 2-11 that products from China, India and Korea lag far behind those of the United States and Japan in the eyes of American consumers. This conclusion is further reinforced when we look at the responses to:

Question: Overall, how do the products produced by Mainland China, India, Japan, and Korea compare to the quality of similar products made in the United States?

TABLE 2-12

(BASE: 297)	PERCENT AGREEMENT		
	Inferior to United States	About the Same	Superior to United States
Chinese products	60	33	3
Indian products	79	16	2
Japanese products	8	50	42
Korean products	54	42	3

As can be seen in Table 2-12, only the products of Japan are considered on a par with, or superior to, U.S.-made products.

Tourism

We also felt that the Chinese government might be interested in the potential for tourism to that country from the United States, so we included a couple of questions on that subject.

As can be seen in Table 2-13, 4 percent of the respondents claim to have visited China. That figure seemed quite high to us, but travel is common among Achievers and the Societally Conscious consumers.

Fifteen percent would actively consider visiting China. That figure is significant and represents yet another justification for an image campaign for China.

TABLE 2-13

COUNTRY/REGION	PERCENT OF AMERICANS WHO HAVE EVER VISITED	PERCENT OF AMERICANS WHO WOULD CONSIDER VISITING
Mexico	51	16
Europe	34	34
Caribbean	27	26
Japan	12	26
Hong Kong	7	8
Korea	5	3
Taiwan	5	3
Australia	5	45
China	4	15
Thailand	4	4
Singapore	3	3
India	0	2

Chap. 2 / Planning the Campaign

06532

DATE:_____

INTERVIEWER:_____

Hello I'm calling long distance for Carol Adams of National Family Opinion, Inc. in Toledo, Ohio. May I please speak to **(AGE AND SEX ON PHONE CARD)** Today I'd like to ask you a few questions about various types of products from different countries.

1. I'm going to read you a list of different countries. For each country, please tell me how familiar you are with the country and the products that country manufactures. After each country, indicate if you are very familiar, somewhat familiar, or not at all familiar with the country and its products. How familiar are you with **(COUNTRY)** and its products? **(REPEAT FOR EACH COUNTRY)**

ROTATE		Very Familiar	Somewhat Familiar	Not At All Familiar
☐	Australia	1	2	3
☐	Caribbean	1	2	3
☐	Mainland China	1	2	3
☐	Europe	1	2	3
☐	Hong Kong	1	2	3
☐	India	1	2	3
☐	Japan	1	2	3
☐	Korea	1	2	3
☐	Mexico	1	2	3
☐	Singapore	1	2	3
☐	Taiwan	1	2	3
☐	Thailand	1	2	3
☐	United States	1	2	3

NATIONAL FAMILY OPINION, INC.
National Family Opinion, Inc. Poll.

2. Now I would like for you to rate these countries on several characteristics pertaining to the quality of its products. Please indicate whether each characteristic describes completely, describes somewhat, or does not describe at all your impression of the country's products.

The first country is (COUNTRY). How well do the following characteristics describe your impression of (COUNTRY'S) products. (REPEAT SCALE AS NECESSARY – READ ENTIRE LIST FOR EACH COUNTRY) (START WITH X'D COUNTRY ABOVE)

ROTATE	CHARACTERISTIC	How Well Describes	☐ Mainland China	☐ India	☐ Japan	☐ Korea	☐ U.S.
☐	There is a high level of craftsmanship in its products	Completely Somewhat Not At All	1 2 3	1 2 3	1 2 3	1 2 3	1 2 3
☐	It produces innovative products	Completely Somewhat Not At All	1 2 3	1 2 3	1 2 3	1 2 3	1 2 3
☐	Has high standards of quality	Completely Somewhat Not At All	1 2 3	1 2 3	1 2 3	1 2 3	1 2 3
☐	Its products sold in the U.S. are a good value	Completely Somewhat Not At All	1 2 3	1 2 3	1 2 3	1 2 3	1 2 3
☐	Use "Old World" techniques in creating its products	Completely Somewhat Not At All	1 2 3	1 2 3	1 2 3	1 2 3	1 2 3
☐	Produce products right for Americans	Completely Somewhat Not At All	1 2 3	1 2 3	1 2 3	1 2 3	1 2 3
☐	Design products reflecting contemporary American tastes	Completely Somewhat Not At All	1 2 3	1 2 3	1 2 3	1 2 3	1 2 3
☐	One can obtain its products in the U.S. at low prices	Completely Somewhat Not At All	1 2 3	1 2 3	1 2 3	1 2 3	1 2 3
☐	Has a wide variety of products easily available in the U.S.	Completely Somewhat Not At All	1 2 3	1 2 3	1 2 3	1 2 3	1 2 3

2b. Overall, how well do the products produced by the following countries compare to the quality of similar products made in the United States? Would you say that (INSERT FIRST COUNTRY)'s products are superior, about the same, or inferior to similar products made in the United States? (REPEAT FOR EACH COUNTRY)

	ROTATE → ☐ Mainland China	☐ India	☐ Japan	☐ Korea
Superior	1	1	1	1
About the same	2	2	2	2
Inferior	3	3	3	3

NATIONAL FAMILY OPINION, INC.

06532

3a. When you think of products produced by **INDIA**, which of the following products do you associate with that country? **(RECORD ONE RESPONSE FOR EACH PRODUCT)**

ROTATE		Yes	No	Don't Know	(DO NOT READ)
☐	Agricultural Equipment	1	N	1	
☐	Silk	2	N	2	
☐	Porcelain	3	N	3	
☐	Furniture	4	N	4	
☐	Clothing	5	N	5	
☐	Handcrafted jewelry	6	N	6	
☐	Consumer electronics (T.V., VCR)	7	N	7	
☐	Scientific Equipment	8	N	8	

3b. What other products from India come to mind?

_____
_____
_____

Any others? **(PROBE UNTIL UNPRODUCTIVE)**

_____
_____
_____

4a. When you think of products produced by **MAINLAND CHINA**, which of the following products do you associate with that country? **(RECORD ONE RESPONSE FOR EACH PRODUCT)**

ROTATE		Yes	No	Don't Know	(DO NOT READ)
☐	Agricultural Equipment	1	N	1	
☐	Silk	2	N	2	
☐	Porcelain	3	N	3	
☐	Furniture	4	N	4	
☐	Clothing	5	N	5	
☐	Handcrafted jewelry	6	N	6	
☐	Consumer electronics (T.V., VCR)	7	N	7	
☐	Scientific Equipment	8	N	8	

4b. What other products from Mainland China come to mind?

_____
_____
_____

Any others? **(PROBE UNTIL UNPRODUCTIVE)**

_____
_____
_____

NATIONAL FAMILY OPINION, INC.   06532

Chap. 2 / Planning the Campaign

5a. When you think of products produced by **JAPAN**, which of the following products do you associate with that country? (RECORD ONE RESPONSE FOR EACH PRODUCT)

ROTATE		Yes	No	Don't Know	(DO NOT READ)
☐	Agricultural Equipment	1	N	1	
☐	Silk	2	N	2	
☐	Porcelain	3	N	3	
☐	Furniture	4	N	4	
☐	Clothing	5	N	5	
☐	Handcrafted jewelry	6	N	6	
☐	Consumer electronics (T.V., VCR) ..	7	N	7	
☐	Scientific Equipment	8	N	8	

5b. What other products from Japan come to mind?

_____
_____
_____

Any others? (PROBE UNTIL UNPRODUCTIVE)

_____
_____
_____

6a. When you think of products produced by **KOREA**, which of the following products do you associate with that country? (RECORD ONE RESPONSE FOR EACH PRODUCT)

ROTATE		Yes	No	Don't Know	(DO NOT READ)
☐	Agricultural Equipment	1	N	1	
☐	Silk	2	N	2	
☐	Porcelain	3	N	3	
☐	Furniture	4	N	4	
☐	Clothing	5	N	5	
☐	Handcrafted jewelry	6	N	6	
☐	Consumer electronics (T.V., VCR) ..	7	N	7	
☐	Scientific Equipment	8	N	8	

6b. What other products from Korea come to mind?

_____
_____
_____

Any others? (PROBE UNTIL UNPRODUCTIVE)

_____
_____
_____

NATIONAL FAMILY OPINION, INC.   06532

7. How likely would you be to consider purchasing a product of India? Would you be . . . (READ LIST)

   Very likely to consider 1
   Somewhat likely to consider 2
   Not very likely to consider, or 3
   Not at all likely to consider 4

8. How likely would you be to consider purchasing a product of Mainland China? Would you be . . . (READ LIST)

   Very likely to consider 1
   Somewhat likely to consider 2   – (SKIP TO QUESTION 9)
   Not very likely to consider, or 3
   Not at all likely to consider 4   – (GO TO QUESTION 8a)

8a. Why not?

   _____
   _____
   _____

9. How likely would you be to consider purchasing a product of Korea? Would you be . . . (READ LIST)

   Very likely to consider 1
   Somewhat likely to consider 2
   Not very likely to consider, or 3
   Not at all likely to consider 4

10. How likely would you be to consider purchasing a product of Japan? Would you be . . . (READ LIST)

    Very likely to consider 1
    Somewhat likely to consider 2
    Not very likely to consider, or 3
    Not at all likely to consider 4

NATIONAL FAMILY OPINION, INC.   06532

Chap. 2 / Planning the Campaign

11. Which of the following countries have you ever visited? (RECORD ONE RESPONSE FOR EACH COUNTRY - RECORD UNDER COLUMN QU. 11 BELOW)
12. Which of these countries would you be most likely to consider visiting? (RECORD ONE RESPONSE FOR EACH COUNTRY - RECORD UNDER COLUMN QU. 12 BELOW)
13. Which of these countries would you definitely not consider visiting? (RECORD ONE RESPONSE FOR EACH COUNTRY - RECORD UNDER COLUMN QU. 13 BELOW)

	Qu. 11 Have Visited		Qu. 12 Consider Visiting		Qu. 13 Not Consider Visiting	
	Yes	No	Yes	No	Yes	No
Australia	01	N	01	N	01	N
Caribbean	02	N	02	N	02	N
Mainland China	03	N	03	N	03	N
Europe	04	N	04	N	04	N
Hong Kong	05	N	05	N	05	N
India	06	N	06	N	06	N
Japan	07	N	07	N	07	N
Korea	08	N	08	N	08	N
Mexico	09	N	09	N	09	N
Singapore	10	N	10	N	10	N
Taiwan	11	N	11	N	11	N
Thailand	12	N	12	N	12	N

14. For each of the following countries, please tell me the capital city of each if you can.

Country	(DO NOT READ RESPONSE)	
Mainland China	Peking/Beijing	1
	Other	2
	Don't Know	3
India	New Delhi	1
	Other	2
	Don't Know	3
Japan	Tokyo	1
	Other	2
	Don't Know	3
Korea	Seoul	1
	Other	2
	Don't Know	3

15. Given the trade deficit of the United States, how likely would you be to boycott products from Japan in the next 12 months? (READ LIST)

    Very likely 1
    Somewhat likely 2
    Might or might not be likely 3
    Somewhat unlikely 4
    Very unlikely 5

16. May I have your age please?

    (WRITE IN) _____ years

17. (RECORD SEX FROM VOICE)

    Male 1

    Female 2

(THANK RESPONDENT AND TERMINATE)

NATIONAL FAMILY OPINION, INC.

06532

CONCLUSIONS

Memorandum

Bozell, Jacobs, Kenyon & Eckhardt, Inc.
Advertising

MEMO TO: Jaye S. Niefeld

FROM: Renee Fraser

RE: Chinese Silk Research

Herewith the findings from the research. As you can see, the conclusions are:

1. Half of the people in the U.S. sample are unfamiliar with China.

2. Among the U.S. consumers, China's products are known for craftsmanship and being made using "Old World" techniques. There is little knowledge of their quality, extent to which they are appropriate for American tastes, their availability, and whether they represent good value.

3. People most willing to consider buying Chinese products tend to be:

   ...Societally conscious
   ...Living in the western U.S.
   ...Somewhat familiar with China

4. U.S. consumers associate with China:

   ...Silk
   ...Porcelain
   ...Clothing

5. About 15% of the sample are strongly interested in visiting China. Those interested in visiting are similar to those who want to buy Chinese products. They are: societally conscious and living in the western U.S.

6. The biggest obstacles to people purchasing Chinese products are lack of knowledge about the products and the quality of workmanship.

I think that what we learned establishes that an image campaign for China would benefit the sale in the U.S. of traditional Chinese products, such as silk.

In addition, as you thought might be the case, there appears to be a real potential for tourism.

I assume you'll be developing the creative and media strategies from this material.

Best of luck,

Renee Fraser

Chapter 3

The Target Groups

THE IMPORTANCE OF THE TARGET GROUP CONCEPT

Undeniably, the most important first step in the development of an advertising campaign is the definition of the target group. Each aspect of the final campaign—creative development, media plans, public relations programs, and merchandising—is dependent on this first step. How can we expect to develop an effective campaign if we do not know whom we are trying to influence? Even in the area of new products, maximum success is usually achieved when we first define the group or groups for whom we want to develop the new products. This "rifle-shot" approach has become the hallmark of the sophisticated advertiser or advertising agency.

WHEN HEAVY USERS ARE NOT TARGETED

Most times, target groups are people who consume unusually large amounts of the product we are advertising. Heavy users are ruled out as primary targets, however, when

- They are already consuming as much of the product as is likely for anyone to be expected to use, or
- A competitor has cornered the heavy-user group and dislodging that competitor's position is beyond the advertiser's resources.

DEFINING THE TARGET GROUP

The definition of a target group can be made on the basis of several dimensions. These categories include (but are not limited to) geographic, demographic, and psychographic definitions.

Geographic If one were to draw a line east and west through Kansas City, one would expect to be able to sell many more heavy overcoats north of that line than south of it, and much more insecticide south of that line than north of it.

Demographic If one were selling denture cleaners, it is logical to expect to sell far more to people over 50 than to teen-agers.

Psychographic If we were to try to define intuitively the target group for a flowers-by-wire service, we might begin with the hypothesis that people who send flowers tend to be warmer, more sensitive, and more emotional than the average person. However, psychological testing has established that people who send flowers by wire usually are in fact less emotional. They send flowers in order to create an emotional reaction in another person—to manipulate the recipient's feelings. Thus, the appeal that will be most effective with flower senders or potential senders is one that demonstrates the flowers' effect on the person receiving them. As the headline of one magazine ad proclaimed: "Something warm and human and wonderful happens when you send flowers by wire."

THE VALS HIERARCHY

Fortunately, there are syndicated research services that lay out several consumer typologies, thus making it easier for us to define target groups. As I pointed out earlier, one of the more prominent of these research organizations is SRI International, which has developed a typology called VALS (for Values and Lifestyles). The VALS typology divides the population into the following nine groups:

1. *Survivors*—Old, intensely poor, fearful, depressed, despairing, far removed from the cultural mainstream, misfits. This group represents about 4 percent of the adult population.
2. *Sustainers*—Living on the edge of poverty, often unemployed, angry, resentful, streetwise, involved in the underground economy. This group represents about 7 percent of the adult population.
3. *Belongers*—Aging, mostly female, traditional, conventional, contented, sentimental, family-oriented, intensely patriotic, deeply stable. This group is the largest in the typology, accounting for about 38 percent of the adult population.
4. *Emulators*—Youthful, ambitious, status conscious, clerical or skilled blue collar, want to appear successful, to make it big. A relatively small group, accounting for about 10 percent of the adult population.
5. *Achievers*—Middle-aged, more heavily male, most affluent group, leaders, materialistic, self-assured, successful. "Movers and shakers," these people make up over 20 percent of the adult population.
6. *I-Am-Me's*—Young, often students, narcissistic, fiercely independent, individualistic, impulsive, dramatic. Next to the smallest group in the typology, accounting for only 3 percent of the adult population.
7. *Experientials*—Youthful, artistic, seeking direct experience and inner growth. This group accounts for 5 percent of the adult population.
8. *Societally Conscious*—Affluent (second only to Achievers), most highly educated of all VALS types, mature, successful, concerned with social issues, leaders. Account for about 11 percent of the adult population.
9. *Integrateds*—Combine the power of the Achievers with the sensitivity of the Societally Conscious, mature, tolerant, understanding. Represent only about 2 percent of the adult population.

(See Figure 3-1).

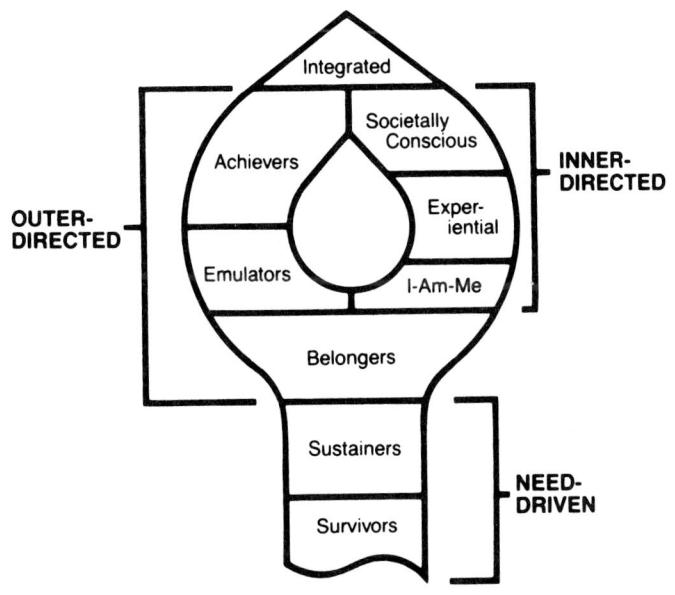

Figure 3-1 A Graphical Representation of the VALS "Hierarchy"

TRANSLATING THE TARGET GROUP INTO A COMPOSITE INDIVIDUAL

An advertisement that addresses an individual is generally more effective than one that addresses a crowd. Therefore, once the target group has been defined, the advertising agency's creative department must translate the target group's characteristics into the image of a single representative consumer. A radio commercial that begins, "Men! At long last you can get relief from razor burn . . ." is unlikely to be as effective as a commercial that begins with, "If you suffer from razor burn. . . ."

ILLUSORY TARGET GROUPS VERSUS MARKETABLE SEGMENTS

In Chapter 2, we referred to a frequent definition of the heavy user of food products, "women 18 to 49 years of age." As we pointed out, this definition is not very useful because no single advertising appeal or media plan would likely be equally effective at each end of this consumer spectrum. Thus, this target-group definition is really an illusory one.

Broad target-group definitions arise because several of the available media ratings services report audience composition data in those terms. It is more convenient and far less costly to use available data, as opposed to conducting the sophisticated research necessary to determine whether age or income or other demographic delineators are even relevant to heavy usage of a product.

The most effective marketing and advertising strategies are based on precise target-group definitions. These definitions allow the development of creative and media executions that are sharply drawn because they are aimed at more or less homogeneous groups.

SOME TYPOLOGIES

As we have indicated, there are several syndicated research services that report on the heavy users of various product categories. Table 3-1 is an example of how one such service (Simmons Market Research Bureau) reports these data.

TABLE 3-1

Simmons Market Research Bureau Report

```
0054                    DRESS: BOUGHT AND NUMBER IN LAST 12 MONTHS                    0054
P-14                                  (FEMALES)                                       P-14
```

	TOTAL U.S. '000	BOUGHT IN LAST 12 MONTHS A '000	B % DOWN	C % ACROSS	D % INDX	LIGHT 1 ITEM A '000	B % DOWN	C % ACROSS	D % INDX	MEDIUM 2-3 ITEMS A '000	B % DOWN	C % ACROSS	D % INDX	HEAVY 4 OR MORE ITEMS A '000	B % DOWN	C % ACROSS	D % INDX
TOTAL FEMALES	91083	35154	100.0	38.6	100	10160	100.0	11.2	100	16471	100.0	18.1	100	8523	100.0	9.4	100
FEMALE HOMEMAKERS	82531	31787	90.4	38.5	100	9141	90.0	11.1	99	15030	91.3	18.2	101	7616	89.4	9.2	99
EMPLOYED MOTHERS	20021	8905	25.3	44.5	115	2306	22.7	11.5	103	4094	24.9	20.4	113	2505	29.4	12.5	134
18 - 24	13762	5401	15.4	39.2	102	1795	17.7	13.0	117	2295	13.9	16.7	92	1311	15.4	9.5	102
25 - 34	21115	8653	24.6	41.0	106	2300	22.6	10.9	98	3822	23.2	18.1	100	2531	29.7	12.0	128
35 - 44	16639	7352	20.9	44.2	114	1901	18.7	11.4	102	3482	21.1	20.9	116	1969	23.1	11.8	126
45 - 54	11704	4898	13.9	41.8	108	1168	11.5	10.0	89	2538	15.4	21.7	120	1192	14.0	10.2	109
55 - 64	11767	4210	12.0	35.8	93	1351	13.3	11.5	103	2004	12.2	17.0	94	855	10.0	7.3	78
65 OR OLDER	16097	4639	13.2	28.8	75	1643	16.2	10.2	92	2331	14.2	14.5	80	665	7.8	4.1	44
18 - 34	34876	14055	40.0	40.3	104	4096	40.3	11.7	105	6117	37.1	17.5	97	3842	45.1	11.0	118
18 - 49	57363	24155	68.7	42.1	109	6558	64.5	11.4	102	11141	67.6	19.4	107	6457	75.8	11.3	120
25 - 54	49458	20904	59.5	42.3	110	5370	52.9	10.9	97	9841	59.7	19.9	110	5692	66.8	11.5	123
35 - 49	22487	10100	28.7	44.9	116	2462	24.2	10.9	98	5024	30.5	22.3	124	2614	30.7	11.6	124
50 OR OLDER	33720	10999	31.3	32.6	85	3602	35.5	10.7	96	5331	32.4	15.8	87	2067	24.3	6.1	66
GRADUATED COLLEGE	13400	6740	19.2	50.3	130	1617	15.9	12.1	108	3199	19.4	23.9	132	1923	22.6	14.4	153
ATTENDED COLLEGE	16826	7967	22.7	47.3	123	2178	21.4	12.9	116	3465	21.0	20.6	114	2323	27.3	13.8	148
GRADUATED HIGH SCHOOL	38408	14022	39.9	36.5	95	4103	40.4	10.7	96	6815	41.4	17.7	98	3104	36.4	8.1	86
DID NOT GRADUATE HIGH SCHOOL	22448	6426	18.3	28.6	74	2262	22.3	10.1	90	2992	18.2	13.3	74	1172	13.8	5.2	56
EMPLOYED FULL-TIME	37461	16689	47.5	44.6	115	4270	42.0	11.4	102	7618	46.3	20.3	112	4801	56.3	12.8	137
EMPLOYED PART-TIME	9494	4321	12.3	45.5	118	1313	12.9	13.8	124	2124	12.9	22.4	124	884	10.4	9.3	100
NOT EMPLOYED	44128	14145	40.2	32.1	83	4577	45.0	10.4	93	6730	40.9	15.3	84	2838	33.3	6.4	69
PROFESSIONAL/MANAGER	11850	6088	17.3	51.4	133	1735	17.1	14.6	131	2744	16.7	23.2	128	1610	18.9	13.6	145
TECH/CLERICAL/SALES	22701	10707	30.5	47.2	122	2675	26.3	11.8	106	4913	29.8	21.6	120	3118	36.6	13.7	147
PRECISION/CRAFT	1196	*567	1.6	47.4	123	**131	1.3	11.0	98	**261	1.6	21.8	121	**176	2.1	14.7	157
OTHER EMPLOYED	11209	3647	10.4	32.5	84	1042	10.3	9.3	83	1824	11.1	16.3	90	781	9.2	7.0	74
SINGLE	16407	6391	18.2	39.0	101	2093	20.6	12.8	114	2733	16.6	16.7	92	1565	18.4	9.5	102
MARRIED	52780	21673	61.7	41.1	106	6039	59.4	11.4	103	10344	62.8	19.6	108	5290	62.1	10.0	107
DIVORCED/SEPARATED/WIDOWED	21896	7090	20.2	32.4	84	2028	20.0	9.3	83	3394	20.6	15.5	86	1668	19.6	7.6	81
PARENTS	33491	13269	37.7	39.6	103	3601	35.4	10.8	96	5956	36.2	17.8	98	3712	43.6	11.1	118
WHITE	78097	30441	86.6	39.0	101	8742	86.0	11.2	100	14432	87.6	18.5	102	7267	85.3	9.3	99
BLACK	10626	3857	11.0	36.3	94	1181	11.6	11.1	100	1735	10.5	16.3	90	942	11.1	8.9	95
OTHER	2360	856	2.4	36.3	94	**237	2.3	10.0	90	*305	1.9	12.9	71	**315	3.7	13.3	143
NORTHEAST-CENSUS	19981	8570	24.4	42.9	111	2099	20.7	10.5	94	4066	24.7	20.3	113	2405	28.2	12.0	129
MIDWEST	22347	8351	23.8	37.4	97	2624	25.8	11.7	105	4114	25.0	18.4	102	1613	18.9	7.2	77
SOUTH	31310	11616	33.0	37.1	96	3500	34.4	11.2	100	5482	33.3	17.5	97	2634	30.9	8.4	90
WEST	17444	6618	18.8	37.9	98	1936	19.1	11.1	99	2810	17.1	16.1	89	1872	22.0	10.7	115
NORTHEAST-MKTG.	20487	8491	24.2	41.4	107	2078	20.5	10.1	91	4095	24.9	20.0	111	2318	27.2	11.3	121
EAST CENTRAL	12885	4752	13.5	36.9	96	1295	12.7	10.1	90	2428	14.7	18.8	104	1029	12.1	8.0	85
WEST CENTRAL	14955	5612	16.0	37.5	97	1815	17.9	12.1	109	2652	16.1	17.7	98	1146	13.4	7.7	82
SOUTH	27091	10271	29.2	37.9	98	3238	31.9	12.0	107	4712	28.6	17.4	96	2321	27.2	8.6	92
PACIFIC	15665	6028	17.1	38.5	100	1735	17.1	11.1	99	2585	15.7	16.5	91	1709	20.1	10.9	117
COUNTY SIZE A	38017	15820	45.0	41.6	108	3798	37.4	10.0	90	7736	47.0	20.3	113	4286	50.3	11.3	120
COUNTY SIZE B	27305	10660	30.3	39.0	101	3276	32.2	12.0	108	4873	29.6	17.8	99	2511	29.5	9.2	98
COUNTY SIZE C	13772	4677	13.3	34.0	88	1428	14.1	10.4	93	2367	14.4	17.2	95	883	10.4	6.4	69
COUNTY SIZE D	11989	3997	11.4	33.3	86	1659	16.3	13.8	124	1496	9.1	12.5	69	843	9.9	7.0	75
METRO CENTRAL CITY	28198	11221	31.9	39.8	103	2803	27.6	9.9	89	5382	32.7	19.1	106	3037	35.6	10.8	115
METRO SUBURBAN	41699	16688	47.5	40.0	104	4657	45.8	11.2	100	8107	49.2	19.4	108	3924	46.0	9.4	101
NON METRO	21186	7245	20.6	34.2	89	2700	26.6	12.7	114	2983	18.1	14.1	78	1562	18.3	7.4	79
TOP 5 ADI'S	20852	9345	26.6	44.8	116	2278	22.4	10.9	98	4544	27.6	21.8	121	2523	29.6	12.1	129
TOP 10 ADI'S	29118	12385	35.2	42.5	110	3072	30.2	10.6	95	5999	36.4	20.6	114	3314	38.9	11.4	122
TOP 20 ADI'S	41659	16978	48.3	40.8	106	4249	41.8	10.2	91	8047	48.9	19.3	107	4682	54.9	11.2	120
HSHLD INC. $60,000 OR MORE	7406	3888	11.1	52.5	136	790	7.8	10.7	96	1933	11.7	26.1	144	1166	13.7	15.7	168
$50,000 OR MORE	12013	6408	18.2	53.3	138	1275	12.5	10.6	95	3254	19.8	27.1	150	1879	22.0	15.6	167
$40,000 OR MORE	22145	11072	31.5	50.0	130	2413	23.7	10.9	97	5390	32.7	24.3	135	3268	38.3	14.8	158
$30,000 OR MORE	36734	17381	49.4	47.3	123	4549	44.8	12.4	111	7878	47.8	21.4	119	4954	58.1	13.5	144
$30,000 - $39,999	14589	6309	17.9	43.2	112	2136	21.0	14.6	131	2488	15.1	17.1	94	1685	19.8	11.5	123
$20,000 - $29,999	18836	7053	20.1	37.4	97	2018	19.9	10.7	96	3605	21.9	19.1	106	1430	16.8	7.6	81
$10,000 - $19,999	19989	6677	19.0	33.4	87	2172	21.4	10.9	97	3062	18.6	15.3	85	1443	16.9	7.2	77
UNDER $10,000	15524	4043	11.5	26.0	67	1420	14.0	9.1	82	1927	11.7	12.4	69	696	8.2	4.5	48
HOUSEHOLD OF 1 PERSON	12984	4093	11.6	31.5	82	1288	12.7	9.9	89	1961	11.9	15.1	84	845	9.9	6.5	70
2 PEOPLE	28049	10796	30.7	38.5	100	3065	30.2	10.9	98	5413	32.9	19.3	107	2318	27.2	8.3	88
3 OR 4 PEOPLE	36053	14814	42.1	41.1	106	4095	40.3	11.4	102	6758	41.0	18.7	104	3960	46.5	11.0	117
5 OR MORE PEOPLE	13997	5452	15.5	39.0	101	1712	16.9	12.2	110	2340	14.2	16.7	92	1400	16.4	10.0	107
NO CHILD IN HSHLD	52195	19705	56.1	37.8	98	5940	58.5	11.4	102	9325	56.6	17.9	99	4441	52.1	8.5	91
CHILD(REN) UNDER 2 YRS	8127	3201	9.1	39.4	102	1006	9.9	12.4	111	1273	7.7	15.7	87	922	10.8	11.3	121
2 - 5 YEARS	13962	5752	16.4	41.2	107	1537	15.1	11.0	99	2706	16.4	19.4	107	1508	17.7	10.8	115
6 - 11 YEARS	17437	7116	20.2	40.8	106	2009	19.8	11.5	103	3128	19.0	17.9	99	1979	23.2	11.3	121
12 - 17 YEARS	17820	6845	19.5	38.4	100	1698	16.7	9.5	85	3420	20.8	19.2	106	1727	20.3	9.7	104
RESIDENCE OWNED	62087	25091	71.4	40.4	105	7084	69.7	11.4	102	11760	71.4	18.9	105	6247	73.3	10.1	108
VALUE: $60,000 OR MORE	33150	14655	41.7	44.2	115	3700	36.4	11.2	100	6953	42.2	21.0	116	4002	47.0	12.1	129
VALUE: UNDER $60,000	28937	10436	29.7	36.1	93	3384	33.3	11.7	105	4807	29.2	16.6	92	2245	26.3	7.8	83

SIMMONS MARKET RESEARCH BUREAU, INC. 1987
*PROJECTION RELATIVELY UNSTABLE BECAUSE OF SAMPLE BASE-USE WITH CAUTION
**NUMBER OF CASES TOO SMALL FOR RELIABILITY-SHOWN FOR CONSISTENCY ONLY

© 1987 By Simmons Market Research Bureau, Inc. All Rights Reserved

Courtesy Simmons Market Research Bureau.

Chap. 3 / The Target Groups

HOW TO READ THE SMRB REPORT

The first column shows the total U.S. population for each demographic category listed. As is pointed out, there are 37,461,000 females in the United States who are employed full time.

Column A is the projected number of people in the specified demographic category who have purchased the product being measured. For example, 16,689,000 of the women who bought a dress in the last twelve months are employed full time.

Column B is the information in column A described as a percentage of the base. Reading down, we see that of all the women who bought a dress in the last twelve months, 47.5 percent are employed full time.

Column C refers to the composition of each demographic category. While "dresses bought in the last twelve months" was the base in column B, the demographic categories are the base in column C. For example, 44.6 percent of the females employed full time have bought a dress in the last twelve months.

Column D is an index of selectivity calculated by dividing the percentage in column C (for the demographic category) by the percentage in column C, the appropriate universe (e.g., adults, males, females). In this case, dividing the 44.6 percent (females employed full time who bought a dress in the last twelve months) by 38.6 percent (total females who bought a dress in the same time period) results in an index of 115. This means that females employed full time were 15 percent more likely to buy a dress than was the average female.

The major disadvantage of this kind of syndicated report is its dependence on demographic data. Often other variables are far more significant.

Audience-Composition Data

While the syndicated research services report on the usage patterns of the population to give us some idea of the makeup of the heavy-user groups, they also give us the audience composition of various media. Advertising agencies then try to reconcile both sets of data and then factor in the cost element. The result is a media plan that reaches the appropriate audience at the most cost-effective level.

Table 3-2 (on p. 36) illustrates how Nielsen, a national television ratings service, provides audience-composition data.

HOW TO READ THE NIELSEN REPORT

The first column of Table 3-2 specifies the details of the program being measured. By using *Newhart* as an example, we see that it is telecast on Monday nights at 9:00 P.M. on CBS. The show, a situation comedy (CS), is thirty minutes in length, and it airs on 212 stations that reach 99 percent of TV households.

The **Key** section breaks viewership down by different periods. Key A is simply the average audience-rating share for the individual week and projected number of viewers (May 2–8). Key B refers to the quarter-to-date viewership, which in this case is April to date (quarter 2). Key C denotes the season-to-date viewership. This period measures the program from its premiere in the fall.

The **Household Audiences** section provides the rating (avg. aud. %), the share (percent of households using television at the time), and the average audience in millions of viewers. For the week of May 2–8, 13.4 percent of TV

TABLE 3-2

PROGRAM AUDIENCE ESTIMATES (Alpha)

MAY 2-8, 1988

VIEWERS PER 1000 VIEWING HOUSEHOLDS BY SPECIFIED CATEGORIES

PROGRAM NAME DAY TIME DUR NET NO. OF #STNS CVG% TYPE T/C	KEY	HOUSEHOLD AUDIENCES AVG.AUD%	AVG.SH%	AVG.AUD.000	TOTAL PERS (2+)	WORKING WOMEN 18+	WORKING WOMEN 18-49	LOH 18-49 W/CH <3	WOMEN TOTAL	W 18-34	W 18-49	W 18-54	W 25-54	W 35-64	W 55+	MEN TOTAL	M 18-34	M 18-49	M 18-54	M 25-54	M 35-64	M 55+	TEENS TOT 12-17	TEENS 12-17	TEENS FEM 12-17	CHILDREN TOT 2-11	CHILDREN TOT 6-11

EVENING CONT'D

NBC MONDAY NIGHT MOVIES-CONT'D
9.30 - 10.00 A 19.7 30 1745 1603 304 245 79 787 275 500 472 384 222 533 197 342 321 262 146 126 66 101
10.00 - 10.30 A 20.9 33 1852 1623 314 254 86 800 287 521 490 399 211 558 210 372 345 282 140 124 59 157 90
10.30 - 11.00 A 20.6 34 1825 1611 326 264 87 811 288 527 499 406 217 581 218 396 364 297 140 113 52 141 64

NBC SUNDAY NIGHT MOVIE
SUN 9.00P 120 NBC 7
 A 19.4 31 1719 1840 327 294 103 754 313 542 477 352 162 764 354 598 514 347 129 170 80 151 82
 B 15.7 25 1388 1658 325 257 80 792 261 476 445 382 260 591 234 395 357 273 161 143 78 131 81
 C 16.5 26 1458 1720 334 272 88 790 304 506 451 355 233 629 260 429 388 288 156 161 86 140 91

SOMETHING IS OUT THERE, PT. 1 203 99 FF 29
9.00 - 9.30 A 18.3 29 1621 1878 326 288 109 768 306 536 479 362 181 760 363 588 513 332 133 187 86 163 91
9.30 - 10.00 A 20.0 31 1772 1856 322 294 101 758 306 537 476 358 171 768 350 594 517 352 134 178 88 152 82
10.00 - 10.30 A 20.1 32 1781 1826 330 298 101 745 317 544 475 346 151 762 351 603 519 353 122 166 78 153 84
10.30 - 11.00 A 19.2 32 1701 1801 328 297 101 747 324 551 480 343 146 767 353 607 506 352 121 151 67 135 72

NEWHART
MON 9.00P 30 CBS 5
 A 13.4 21 1187 1543 341 274 84 777 289 485 458 339 245 497 190 322 321 230 133 114 53 155 104
 B 14.0 22 1244 1589 349 284 96 795 301 503 456 336 254 534 190 342 339 259 152 108 56 153 96
 C 16.2 24 1433 1606 357 287 98 830 301 490 459 350 289 538 196 342 329 255 165 101 56 136 85

NIGHT COURT 212 99 CS 29
 A 21.7 35 1923 1624 320 276 113 727 310 495 466 304 188 579 257 422 383 255 128 150 81 168 98

THU
 B 21.7 35 1923 1624 320 276 113 727 310 495 466 304 188 579 257 422 383 255 128 150 81 168 98
 C 21.7 35 1923 1624 320 276 113 727 310 495 466 304 188 579 257 422 383 255 128 150 81 168 98

OHARA(R)
SAT 9.00P 60 ABC 7
200 97 OP 14
 A 6.3 12 558 1595 247 168 43^ 762 109^ 297 331 397 404 569 84^ 214 225 321 301 108^ 47^ 156 96^
 B 7.6 14 672 1668 283 199 52 794 158 369 385 426 362 611 136 303 307 335 258 82 34^ 180 113
 A 8.3 14 733 1688 289 212 58 790 165 384 400 423 344 639 147 331 337 346 256 88 38 171 115
 B 5.6 11 496 1577 249 171 36^ 758 103^ 294 329 399 402 559 70^ 193 220 325 309 99^ 38^ 160 106^
 C 6.9 13 611 1633 249 167 49^ 776 116 304 337 401 411 584 96^ 234 232 323 299 116 55^ 156 90^

OUR HOUSE
SUN 7.00P 60 NBC 6
202 99 GD 29
 A 7.1 15 629 1715 249 197 34^ 809 187 395 376 392 362 532 136 251 227 262 237 184 83^ 190 148
 B 7.8 15 694 1643 274 208 41^ 774 190 372 355 357 345 486 145 252 229 200 148 159 95 224 168
 C 11.0 18 977 1800 322 259 65 806 238 437 413 366 315 563 189 336 315 273 181 168 92 263 185
7.00 - 7.30 A 11.9 22 1052 1688 240 188 36^ 812 185 390 370 380 367 539 139 370 240 256 245 175 75^ 162 122
7.30 - 8.00 A 7.6 15 673 1717 253 203 32^ 797 187 395 377 370 353 520 132 247 250 264 227 189 88^ 211 168

PERFECT STRANGERS
FRI 8.00P 30 ABC 7
212 99 CS 10
 A 9.8 20 868 1684 273 212 104 845 258 452 444 360 332 448 180 262 240 179 155 95 52^ 297 188
 B 11.4 22 1008 1634 279 211 88 788 247 412 394 325 324 462 169 278 260 215 149 130 79 254 158
 C 11.9 22 1052 1665 279 218 94 789 257 427 409 330 307 460 170 276 261 213 147 135 81 281 177

PRESIDENTIAL PORTRAIT
MON&THU 9.58P 1 CBS 16
210 98 DO 77
 A 12.6 20 1116 1540 327 248 85 868 259 463 452 402 335 482 158 272 274 221 171 73 39 117 73
 B 12.7 21 1129 1557 311 238 76 827 248 445 429 387 326 507 168 284 274 237 184 92 44 131 76
 C 13.0 21 1149 1579 319 239 73 846 239 440 426 399 346 528 162 289 279 257 201 91 45 114 70

TUE 10.00P 1
9.30 - 10.00 A 11.4 18 1010 1512 328 257 81 848 265 454 441 372 331 475 171 266 274 213 163 76 37^ 114 74
10.00 - 10.30 A 15.0 24 1329 1583 324 235 90 900 251 478 469 448 342 491 138 255 269 232 184 70 42 122 72

A=CURRENT REPORT B=QUARTER AVERAGE C=SEASON AVERAGE

FOR EXPLANATION OF SYMBOLS, SEE PAGE B.

Courtesy Nielsen Media Research.

households watched *Newhart* (11,870,000 viewers), and this represented 21 percent of all households using television.

The remainder of Table 3-2 provides information on **Viewers per 1,000 Viewing Households** by demographic categories. The first breakdown measures total persons (aged 2+), working women 18+ and 18–49 years of age, and "ladies of the household" (LOH) with children under age 3. The next two categories define women and men viewers under five age breakdowns. The final two categories measure teens and children. In this case,

- An average of 96,000 ladies of the household (LOH) with children under 3 years of age have watched *Newhart* from the beginning of the quarter (April) to date (key B).
- An average of 459,000 women aged 25–54 have watched *Newhart* since its premiere last fall (key C).
- An average of 114,000 teens aged 12–17 watched *Newhart* the week of May 2–8 (key A).

In the search for more sophisticated definitions of target groups, the PRIZM Cluster System* has delineated forty categories, based on census data. Essentially, this research organization has combined demographic information to create the following lifestyle categories:

TABLE 3-3

CLUSTER NICKNAMES	PERCENT OF U.S. HOUSEHOLDS	PERCENT GROUPS
Blue Blood Estates	0.84	
Money & Brains	0.99	
Furs & Station Wagons	2.90	4.73
Pools & Patios	3.66	
Two More Rungs	0.85	
Young Influentials	2.63	7.14
Young Suburbia	5.53	
Blue-Chip Blues	6.18	11.71
Urban Gold Coast	0.50	
Bohemian Mix	1.16	
Black Enterprise	0.75	
New Beginnings	5.16	7.57
God's Country	2.39	
New Homesteaders	4.76	
Towns & Gowns	1.37	8.52
Levittown, U.S.A.	3.29	
Gray Power	2.09	
Rank & File	1.36	6.74
Blue-Collar Nursery	2.40	
Middle America	3.54	
Coalburg & Corntown	2.01	7.95

* PRIZM is a registered trademark of Claritas Corporation.

TABLE 3-3 (Continued)

CLUSTER NICKNAMES	PERCENT OF U.S. HOUSEHOLDS	PERCENT GROUPS
New Melting Pot	0.95	
Old Yankee Rows	1.84	
Emergent Minorities	1.77	
Single City Blues	2.75	7.31
Shotguns & Pickups	1.82	
Agri-Business	2.56	
Grain Belt	1.19	5.57
Golden Ponds	5.06	
Mines & Mills	2.60	
Norma Rae-Ville	2.77	
Smalltown Downtown	2.73	13.16
Back-Country Folks	3.16	
Share Croppers	3.75	
Tobacco Roads	1.08	
Hard Scrabble	1.04	9.03
Heavy Industry	2.50	
Downtown Dixie-Style	3.49	
Hispanic Mix	1.94	
Public Assistance	2.65	10.58
TOTAL U.S.	100.00	100.00

CONSUMER TARGETS FOR CHINESE SILK

Our consumer research disclosed that porcelain and silk are the products that Americans most closely associate with China. We felt that silk offered a wider variety of applications than porcelain and therefore would yield a greater number of interesting advertisements. Silk is used for clothing, accessories, draperies, furniture covers, even cosmetics. Each of these product types has its own target group. The heaviest use for silk, however, is for clothing. Therefore, we decided to concentrate our advertising on apparel. Specifically, we chose as the focus of our advertising campaign dresses and blouses for women and suits for men.

By referring to available research sources, we sought to define the appropri-

TABLE 3-4

Index of Dresses Bought in Last Twelve Months
(100 = Average for All Women)

VALS TYPE	ONE DRESS	TWO TO THREE DRESSES	FOUR+ DRESSES
Survivors	44	41	29
Sustainers	74	39	53
Belongers	102	93	64
Emulators	93	106	99
Achievers	108	143	(168)
I-Am-Me's	118	132	108
Experientials	120	116	(148)
Societally Conscious	118	110	(175)

ate target groups and emerged with a VALS definition. This research was conducted by SRI in its annual survey and is based on a sample of approximately 1,500 respondents. As can be seen in Table 3-4, Achievers, Experientials, and the Societally Conscious were the heaviest purchasers of dresses. Women in these groups on average were 68, 48, and 75 percent more likely to buy four or more dresses per year than was the average woman.

As for the purchase of men's suits, it was Achievers (more than twice as likely as the average man to buy three or more suits a year) and the Societally Conscious (27 percent more likely) who emerged as the most logical targets.

TABLE 3-5

Index of Men's Winter or All-Year Suits
Bought in Last Twelve Months
(100 = Average for All Men)

VALS TYPE	ONE SUIT	TWO SUITS	THREE+ SUITS
Survivors	10	64	7
Sustainers	57	30	95
Belongers	73	48	34
Emulators	49	86	45
Achievers	149	148	(216)
I-Am-Me's	72	96	101
Experientials	89	297	54
Societally Conscious	166	125	(127)

VALS has interviewed consumers who represent each category in their typology. Here are some excerpts from the interviews with Belongers, Achievers, and the Societally Conscious—to give the reader an idea of what these groups are like:

BELONGERS

Dave: I think America is the greatest place in the world to live. I don't think there's any place better [except] when we die and go to heaven if you're a Christian.

Narrator: We know these people, the stiff backbone of America. They get a job, and they stick with it.

Donna: Maybe I'm old-fashioned, but I don't like change all that much.

Narrator: More than a third of us are Belongers. The people who work eight to five and bring the money home. The strong middle that keeps God, country, and family central to American life.

Dave: It's important to us. We want to have a close family. If you're not happy at home, where are you going to be happy . . . ? That's the way I feel.

Donna: It seems like it was easier when I was working, but I need to be home. I feel that it's my place because when I was growing up, when I came home, my Mom was always there, and that's how I want it to be for my kids.

Narrator: The often discussed change in American morals hasn't really penetrated here. These people are very clear about right and wrong.

Dave: I think that you have to know what's right and wrong to be able to live with [yourself]. Because I don't want [my kids] to grow up and be criminals or people like when they hold a job, they can't be trusted. Or people won't work with them because they lie or they cheat . . . . You won't be right with the Lord if you're not honest.

ACHIEVERS

Steve: When I graduated from Columbia Law School, my main desire was to get into the business world but not particularly as an attorney.

Narrator: The Emulator's dream is probably Ann-Marie and Steve. Sleek and chic, these are the folks bathed in the winter's glow.

Steve: I did practice law for a couple of years just to make sure, since I had invested all the time and energies into law school. After a few years, I found out that basically I was not cut out just to be an attorney but wanted to be more of an entrepreneur. It's probably every entrepreneur's goal to be financially successful, but basically [money's] simply a way of keeping score. It's not the end result. I think for me it was more to be independent. To be able to do what I chose to do, to live my own lifestyle, to have my own hours. Not to be beholden to somebody else's desires or wishes.

Narrator: This is the one-fifth of Americans who are decisive, driving, and driven. They put in enough time at the right places. They have the right stuff. Achievers know what they want professionally, socially, and materially, and they make it happen.

Ann-Marie: Having a nice home, having enough room, having independence, having luxuries, things that I believe the common mortal [does not run] into every day. Being able to collect things that I like, having the space to put them, and for them to be seen. To be able to live a life of what I would call luxury.

Narrator: The . . . classic American dream is their reality. Rewards are visible and external. Achievers are satisfied with their place in society.

SOCIETALLY CONSCIOUS

Narrator: Many in this group have stepped past the corporate ladder. They are people combining work with a passion for social change. People like Tom. Top of his class at Harvard Law School, Tom's been working through a clutter of cases at the Environmental Defense Fund for twelve years. He lives a life of simple pleasures. He does not have many material possessions. He has his work, his family, and his commitments.

Tom: I sometimes feel like I'm not doing my share. I mean particularly on an issue like weapons proliferation and arms control. Some of the people are putting their lives on the line. I sometimes think I should be there rather than here.

Sherona: We have a lot of friends who are very, very well-to-do, and I think when we go to their houses [we experience] a mixture of a little envy and a little contempt, too. They make money for big companies . . . and for themselves while they're at it. They do very little that's at all socially reforming.

Tom: I earn a pretty good living so I don't feel I'm sacrificing a whole lot, but I think there are other values, in addition to making a good income, which are important. One of those is trying to do something that's socially useful and maybe makes the world a little better place.

OUR FIVE-TARGET-GROUP APPROACH

Consumers are only one of the Chinese silk target groups. In order to understand the dynamics of the sale of Chinese silk, it is necessary to understand the *selling process* in the American garment industry. In America, fashion is a five-step process:

Chap. 3 / The Target Groups 41

Figure 3-2 The Designer

First, the **designer** (Figure 3-2) conceives the idea of the garment, then specifies the look of the garment and finally the materials that will be used. Prototypes of the garment are then made by the designer. An entire collection of the designer's fashion ideas are assembled and presented to clothing buyers for one or more retail stores.

As for the designer's perception of Chinese silk, Ralph Lauren—one of the world's most successful designers who also owns many retail stores in major cities throughout the world — had this to say:

> I try to understand the various customers I design for. What will make each person feel better about herself or himself? What are the lifestyle trends that will have an impact on the way the customer lives, and how will clothes fit into those lifestyle trends?
>
> And then I want to offer things that are unusual and that have class. Things that are aesthetically pleasing.
>
> Interestingly, Chinese silk can be all of those things—unusual, classy, and aesthetically pleasing. And if various segments of the American public are shown designs that fit into their lifestyles, the potential for Chinese silk can be very great.

Second, the **retail buyers** (Figure 3-3) place orders with the designer. They order the items they feel will sell best to their customers.

Third, the orders are assembled by the designer and sent off to the **manufacturer** (Figure 3-4) to be produced.

Figure 3-3 The Retail Buyer

Fourth, the manufacturer sends the finished items directly to the **retailer**. Here, the items are priced and displayed on the sales floor (Figure 3-5) for purchase.

Finally, **customers** (Figure 3-6) select those items that suit their tastes, their fabric preferences, and their budgets.

Figure 3-4 The Manufacturer
Photograph courtesy of Benno Gross Associates Ltd.

Figure 3-5 The Retail Floor

Figure 3-6 The Retail Customer

43

To summarize, our five target groups are

1. The designer who presents his or her ideas to the retail buyers,
2. The buyers for the retail stores,
3. The manufacturers of the ordered apparel,
4. The retailers who receive the ordered merchandise, and
5. The consumer.

Chapter 4

Media

The Beijing presentation was not set up to discuss media programs in any detail. The audience was not familiar with available U.S. media, and the time allotted was insufficient for a thorough analysis of media. Thus, the presentation's media section was more illustrative than definitive.

Our Chinese advisors indicated that it would be inappropriate to tie ourselves to a firm budget figure for the presentation. They stated that culturally the Chinese are accustomed to considerable flexibility in their working relationships. Accordingly, they suggested that we present a *number* of alternatives (a maximum amount of $10 million to a minimum amount of $300,000) relative to media budget. Because the Chinese prefer to work with multiple alternatives, they felt this kind of approach would play quite well with the audience. They also stressed that the presentation should be broad in nature. The audience would be lost if we bogged down in details.

MEDIA OBJECTIVES

Our basic media objectives were to

1. Cover a large number of our target group, and
2. Use our limited media dollars to generate additional money for the advertising of China and Chinese silk.

Tackling the media problems proved challenging but not insurmountable. We looked at the available syndicated media research to determine which media would reach our five target audiences: (1) designers; (2) manufacturers of apparel; (3) retailer buyers; (4) retailers; and (5) consumers.

Please note that these were very specific and marketable target groups, not illusory targets. Various groups in the chain of distribution, combined with the VALS consumer groups recapitulated on p. 47, made up the very narrowly defined targets we sought to reach.

Memorandum

Bozell, Jacobs, Kenyon & Eckhardt, Inc.
Advertising

MEMO TO: James Spero

FROM: Jaye S. Niefeld

RE: Beijing Conference

Confirming this morning's telephone conversation, Jim, you're going to undertake the planning of a media program for our China image campaign and the accompanying Chinese silk campaign.

You already know about the tight budgets, so you'll work with P.R. to develop the best program you can come up with for the dollars. Our Hong Kong advisors have suggested three plans -- at the $300,000 level and at the $5 million and $10 million levels. I really think that is too much to cover in our presentation and too much money at the $5 million and $10 million figures. Let's just use the $300,000 budget and one at $3,000,000 -- unless you can justify and substantiate a dollar figure at some other level.

Don't burden yourself with providing much detail. The audience we're presenting to will neither want nor need a detailed media proposal.

Thanks for taking on this assignment, Jim. I know it represents a lot of extra effort for your department.

All the best,

Chap. 4 / Media

TABLE 4-1

Index of Dresses Bought in Last Twelve Months
(100 = Average for All Women)

VALS TYPE	ONE DRESS	TWO TO THREE DRESSES	FOUR+ DRESSES
Survivors	44	41	29
Sustainers	74	39	53
Belongers	102	93	64
Emulators	93	106	99
Achievers	108	143	(168)
I-Am-Me's	118	132	108
Experientials	120	116	(148)
Societally Conscious	118	110	(175)

TABLE 4-2

Index of Men's Winter or All-Year Suits
Bought in Last Twelve Months
(100 = Average for All Men)

VALS TYPE	ONE SUIT	TWO SUITS	THREE+ SUITS
Survivors	10	64	7
Sustainers	57	30	95
Belongers	73	48	34
Emulators	49	86	45
Achievers	149	148	(216)
I-Am-Me's	72	96	101
Experientials	89	297	54
Societally Conscious	166	125	(127)

Happily, an easily identifiable group of fashion publications reaches all of our target groups. The magazines most appropriate to our mission were

Harper's Bazaar	721,000 circulation
Vogue	1,260,000 circulation
W	226,000 circulation

(See Figure 4-1).

Other magazines to be considered should a larger budget become available were

MAGAZINE	CIRCULATION
McCall's	5,349,181
Women's Day	5,263,894
Time	4,600,000
Playboy	3,672,063
Newsweek	3,181,187
People	2,892,137
Cosmopolitan	2,864,343
ELLE	721,269
Esquire	702,611
Shape	678,349
GQ	667,105
Ms	481,466
M	137,018

Figure 4-1 Three Fashion Magazines

These publications have both the audiences and editorial environment appropriate to the sale of Chinese silk.

Although other publications might be used, our limited budget led us to narrow the field to the three listed on page 47. To create the proper effect, however, we felt that large space advertisements were desirable. Because large space ads are expensive, we needed to find a way to pay for them. Our strategy was to create an additional budget for Chinese silk advertising. That additional budget would come from the various target groups—designers, manufacturers, and retailers—interested in furthering the sale of this glamourous product.

The additional dollars would be spent in the media that reached these groups as well as consumers. If enough additional money was generated, we felt it might well be invested in television advertising. Showing silk apparel as part of everyday life would create a highly desirable visual impact.

Event Media

Our agency's approach to media budget allocation directs that we place roughly 80 percent of the budget into media that achieve the advertiser's reach and frequency goals in the most cost-efficient manner. That might include pages or even fractional pages in newspapers and/or magazines or thirty-second television and/or radio spots. According to this philosophy, the approximately 20 percent of the budget remaining should be spent to create sheer impact; that is, special events, special programming, and multipage units, without undue concern for cost-efficiencies. The following are some examples of this approach:

1. We devoted the back pages of the four sections of the *New York Times* on a single day to four full-page ads for *Business Week* magazine.

2. With the cooperation of *Fortune*, we caused the publication of an extra (twenty-seventh) edition of that magazine, in which all of the advertising consisted of Merrill Lynch ads.

This event media concept allows the budget to respond to (1) the purely statistical data dealing with reach and frequency and (2) the element of emotional impact having to do more with persuasion than with either reach or frequency. In addition to the media alternatives for the China image campaign listed above, television commercials would be prepared, which local retailers might air in connection with any store promotions that included products from China or, more specifically, Chinese silk.

Minimum Media Budget: $300,000

As mentioned previously, it is not our intent to discuss media programs in any detail. We will simply indicate the kinds of media alternatives that exist at two different budget levels.

Although we wanted to reach many millions of consumers, a $300,000 budget was simply not adequate. The best way to approach the problem seemed to be *not* to spend the budget on conventional advertising. Instead, the money should be used as a means to generate more advertising dollars that would be contributed by American fashion companies. This approach had three parts.

A. We would use part of the $300,000 to develop a series of in-store promotions in a number of the best department stores (e.g., Neiman Marcus, Marshall Field's, Saks Fifth Avenue, and Bloomingdale's).
B. Another part of our budget would be spent to assist the stores in putting together multipage advertising units, which would be paid for by the designers and manufacturers who supplied these stores. These multipage units would run in the important fashion magazines mentioned earlier in this chapter.

These fashion magazines are ostensibly designed to reach consumers, but in reality, they are a cross between consumer advertising and trade advertising. The magazines are accustomed to publishing special sections and multipage units from both manufacturers and retailers.

C. The third portion of the budget would be used by the Silk Commission of the People's Republic of China to secure contributions toward multipage ads directly from designers and manufacturers. These insertions could then be used in newspapers, fashion magazines, and more general magazines.

In addition, the Chinese government could make available, at virtually no hard-currency costs, an array of Chinese fashion models as their contribution to the designers and manufacturers. The promotion opportunities are endless: traveling fashion shows, television specials, talk show appearances, and so on, perhaps even a syndicated television special.

If the Chinese were interested in the European market, the same idea could be used in *ELLE* magazine, *Paris Match*, *English Bazaar*, and others. It was easy to visualize the Chinese fashion models in such cosmopolitan cities as Paris or Milan.

A More Typical Budget: $3 Million

If we had a more typical budget for advertising in the United States, say $3 million, we could deliver a considerable audience to the allure of Chinese silk.

Our media program would include, in addition to *Vogue*, *Harper's Bazaar*, and *W*, multipage inserts in

People	Woman's Day
Newsweek	Shape
GQ	Elle
Esquire	McCall's
M	Ms.
Playboy	Cosmopolitan

(See Figure 4-2.)

We would also present our advertising in the highest-rated prime time television programs.

This budget level would reach approximately 70 percent of our target groups an average of four times a year.

Figure 4-2 High Circulation Magazines

Chapter 5

Public Relations

Rather than using conventional paid advertising, we frequently write and place articles and other featured material in the media as a means to publicize a client's service or product. These public relations activities have several advantages over advertising.

1. They frequently offer objective, third-party endorsement.
2. They often run to several pages in a publication or several minutes in a broadcast, as opposed to the more modest lengths typical of print advertising or broadcast commercials.
3. Because the material appears as editorial matter, the claims or descriptions or documentation of the company (or product or service) are perceived as more credible.
4. Public relations activities are almost always substantially less expensive than equivalent amounts of paid advertising.

There is another side to this issue, though. There are substantial disadvantages to public relations activities when compared with advertising:

1. The company has no control over what will finally be printed or aired. Indeed, it happens more than occasionally that the stories or features that finally run are negative in tone rather than complimentary.
2. The company frequently has no control over the timing of the stories or other public relations activities.

In light of the very modest budget for advertising China and Chinese silk, it is important that our communication plan should include a public relations program. Following is an outline of our ideas for a public relations plan for

Memorandum

Bozell, Jacobs, Kenyon & Eckhardt, Inc.
Advertising

MEMO TO: Ward White

FROM: Terry Gruggen

RE: Beijing Conference Public Relations Section

Thanks, Ward, for assigning Bob Bagar to the Beijing project. Please keep in mind that the Chinese government has very little hard-currency reserves, so you'll have to develop a P.R. program to augment the very small media budget.

The best way might be to come up with a market-by-market approach rather than a national program, and we'd go into as many cities as the Chinese could afford.

We're really under the gun in terms of time. I'd appreciate it if we could get your recommendations in two weeks. I'm enclosing the target-group descriptions and strategies, as well as some interesting information on Chinese silk. Hope it's useful.

I really appreciate your help.

Best wishes,

Ward White was president of Bozell, Jacobs, Kenyon & Eckhardt public relations division.

CHINA PROJECT

Assignment:
    Presentation of an advertising campaign illustrating how an image campaign for China in the West would in turn have beneficial effects on all products made in China.

Tentative Strategy # 1
    -- China image campaign:

    China has a 5000 year tradition of craftsmanship dedicated to the creating of products known for their beauty and quality. This tradition is seen dramatically in such products as silk, ivory, porcelain, jade, sculpture, and rugs.

Tentative Strategy # 2
    -- Pure Chinese silk:

    Today, as it has been for almost 5000 years, silk is treasured as a unique, beautiful and luxurious fabric - used in the most prestigious products. Consumers who wish the very best prefer pure Chinese silk, which is why more of this rare textile comes from China than from all of the 34 other silk-producing countries combined.

Targets:
    Because of its uniqueness, expensiveness, and naturalness, our campaign should be directed to:

    Achievers (about 20% of U.S.)
    Societally Conscious (about 12%)

Silk Products:

Dresses	Tapestries
Suits	Quilts and Comforters
Blouses and Shirts	Kimonos
Hosiery	Saris
Women's hats	Accessories
Rugs	Kites

    Also such non-traditional uses as:

    Tennis-racket strings
    Fly-fishing lines
    Silk-based cold cream
    Bicycle tires
    Surgical sutures
    Dolls
    Nose-covering for the Concorde

Why Chinese Silk?
> Most of the cultivated silk we use, even that from Italy and France, originates in China, which produces more than half the world's (supply).

Some of the words used to describe silk:
> Lustrous, luxurious, seductive, splendor, shimmering, mysterious, enchanting, unique, miraculous, natural fiber, sensual, sensuous, sexy, living, lovely, intricate, exquisite, exciting, romantic, elegant.

Some interesting facts about silk:
1. Many Chinese and Indian designs in silk go back over 1,000 years.
2. Many famous people, including royalty, loved silk clothes and other items. These include: Alexander the Great, Napoleon, Catherine the Great, Pope Julius II, Sigurd the Crusader (King of Norway), and even today, the Empress of Japan, the Queen of England, etc.
3. Legend attributes the secret of silk to Chinese Empress Xi Ling Shi in the year 2640 B.C. - over 4,600 years ago.
4. For hundreds of years, the secret of silk was guarded: Chinese imperial law decreed death by torture to those who disclosed it.
5. The prophet Ezekial mentions silk in the Old Testament. Indeed, Chotalal Salvi, an Indian silk producer has said, "Silk is the holy cloth. It is what you wear if you want to touch God."
6. In Julius Caesar's time, silk was worth its weight in gold.
7. The Silk Road was 4,000 miles long and was traversed by caravans almost 2,000 years ago. In the 13th century, Marco Polo traveled the Silk Road and brought silk to Venice.
8. Islam carried silk from the Middle East across North Africa to Spain in about the 9th century.
9. Later, the Crusaders brought back to Europe silks they acquired in the Middle East.
10. In the 15th century, Italian royalty had silk patterns embroidered in their clothing that had been designed by Leonardo da Vinci for frescoes.

11. Even today, the skills used to make silk are over 1,000 years old.
12. Silk can be very durable. Silk embroidery exists that is 4,500 years old. Silk quilts and gowns 2,300 years old were uncovered in an archeological dig in China.
13. Recently, at least half the models in the Paris haute-couture shows wore silk.
14. Chinese silk yarn is made into Italian fabrics which are revered by dress designers the world over.
15. Diagrams, to look like musical notations, translate design descriptions in directions for weavers.
16. A silk tie requires 20 steps to produce.
17. Only two-tenths of one percent of the textiles produced in the world are silk.
18. Oscar de la Renta has said: "Silk does for the body what diamonds do for the hand."

Chinese silk. Our work to promote that product in the United States has these main objectives:

1. To increase awareness and appreciation of Chinese silk among American consumers and the fashion industry.
2. To supply authentic, up-to-date information about Chinese silk to major U.S. media outlets so that we can achieve national coverage and create interest and enthusiasm for the product.
3. To reach the more affluent Americans with feature stories that praise Chinese silk.
4. To demonstrate the allure, quality, and superiority of Chinese silk and to show it as a favorite material of the world's leading designers.
5. To influence the continuing use of Chinese silk by America's retailing, manufacturing, and apparel industries and to establish the appeal of Chinese silk among American consumers.

FOCUS OF PUBLIC RELATIONS RELEASES

Public relations offers Chinese commercial interests the opportunity to tell the compelling story of Chinese silk and how well it fits into modern American life. We would develop several public relations releases. These releases would focus on one or several of the virtues of silk. The following topics would be stressed:

1. The romance of silk as demonstrated by today's fashion;
2. Its preference by the world's leading fashion designers;

Figure 5-1 Living with Silk in Apparel, Draperies, Rugs, Upholstery Covers, and Even Silk Flowers and Paintings on Silk

3. The diversity of silk in casual, evening, and business dress as well as intimate wear;
4. Silk products in fabric and textiles that add beauty and style to the home, e.g., in draperies, pillows, rugs, upholstery pieces, and table settings (Figures 5-1, 5-2);
5. The history of Chinese silk, headlining China's status as the world's leading supplier (Figure 5-3);
6. Chinese silk interpreted through the arts and its place in tradition and ritual;
7. New-product applications (e.g., in shampoos, face creams, and other cosmetic products);
8. The attractions of Chinese silk, told from a business perspective.

Resulting stories written by the agency's public relations arm would be placed in influential U.S. business publications that reach manufacturers, designers, retailers, decision makers, and opinion leaders (Figure 5-4). These articles would describe the nature and development of the silk industries and China's global business operation in silk exports.

Figure 5-2 The Creation of Contemporary Chinese Silk Rugs

Figure 5-3 The History of Silk, with Emphasis on the Ancient Silk Caravans

Figure 5-4 Placement in Business Publications

ELEMENTS OF THE STRATEGY

A number of elements would be part of our public relations strategy:

- A "Treasures of China" press kit would be printed (Figure 5-5). The cover, which would show the product logos, would be designed with a silklike texture and color. The paper used for the initial production of press releases would also be silklike to represent the quality of the product. This kit would be distributed to the key editors in the U.S. general, business, consumer, broadcast, and trade press.
- A documentary film on the history of Chinese silk. This film would be made for television audiences from available films on China. The introduction would be produced in China. A film of this kind would reach a wide viewing audience and could also be shown on shopping mall television outlets where millions of American consumers make most of their buying decisions.
- A video news release, prepared from a short version of the Chinese silk story, would be produced in a television news style. This TV report on the silk of China would appear on prime time news spots in major U.S. cities. (See Figure 5-6.)
- A tour of important U.S. cities would be booked. An attractive Chinese lecturer would show examples of exquisite garments, fashionable wom-

Figure 5-5 Press Kit

Figure 5-6 Video News Release

Figure 5-7 Chinese Models Touring the United States

Figure 5-8 Chinese Silk Exhibit in U.S. Shopping Mall

en's wear, and other products made from Chinese silk (Figure 5-7). Interviews with leading newspaper and television reporters would be arranged in advance of these visits.

- A traveling shopping mall exhibition entitled "Treasures of China: Silk" would be prepared for America's leading shopping malls (Figure 5-8). It would consist of color photographs and text panels depicting the entire story of Chinese silk. It would also have on display silk samples, examples of cocoons, and products made of silk. A press preview aimed at coverage that would attract visitors would be held in every exhibit site over the eight-month tour.

This type of activity would generate great product exposure in an influential retail environment. The shopping-mall exhibition could also be tied into special department store promotions of Chinese silk at which a variety of Chinese silk products would be featured.

COST OF THE PUBLIC RELATIONS CAMPAIGN

Implementing a public relations program of this type on a national basis would cost approximately $275,000. However, individual programs of the types we have just mentioned could be implemented in single markets for as little as $5,000 to $10,000 depending on the size of the market. We are confident that this type of public relations program could be very influential in the promotion of Chinese silk to the American consumer.

Chapter 6

The Creative Work

OUTLINING CREATIVE OBJECTIVES

We customarily set creative objectives in the following fashion:

1. *Awareness objectives*
   Advertising must capture the attention of the target group. No matter how persuasive the content of the advertising, it cannot be effective if it does not gain the audience's ear (and eye).

2. *Involvement*
   Next, the advertising must evoke a response from its audience. This response may be an emotional reaction to specific elements of the ad.

3. *Perception*
   Having attracted the attention of the audience, the advertising must then either (a) reinforce favorable attitudes toward the advertised brand or (b) improve brand awareness, recognition, and existing beliefs or images.

4. *Comprehension and Storage*
   An important link in the creative chain is the transmission of information in a clear, unambiguous manner. The optimum result is to have the audience assimilate the content of the advertisement without attributing that message to an advertising source. The information simply goes into the target's general fund of knowledge.

5. *Conviction*
   An effective advertising campaign will persuade its audience to respond favorably to the advertised product or service.

Memorandum

Bozell, Jacobs, Kenyon & Eckhardt, Inc.
Advertising

MEMO TO: John LaPick

FROM: Jaye S. Niefeld

RE: Beijing Advertising Conference

This memo is to confirm our telephone conversation. I'm enclosing several articles which the Corporate Information Center has dug up - on China and Chinese silk. The article from the National Geographic is particularly good.

This information is just to provide your Creatives with background for the project. Before proceeding with any specific creative work, wait until we provide you with some of the findings from the research we're conducting. That research should yield creative strategies, both consumer and trade.

We expect the research to be completed by April 1, and you will have the material and the strategies within a week after that.

This project should be an exciting assignment for your group, John, and I'm looking forward to working with you on it.

Cordially,

[signature]

John LaPick was creative director of the agency's Los Angeles office.

Memorandum

Bozell, Jacobs, Kenyon & Eckhardt, Inc.
Advertising

MEMO TO: John LaPick

FROM: Jaye S. Niefeld

RE: Creative Strategies for Chinese Silk Campaign

I know you've been anxious for the creative strategies. Actually, there are four sets of strategies, each aimed at a different target group:

1. <u>Fashion designers.</u> To designers of clothing we wish to convey the understanding that Chinese silk looks good; is of the highest quality; is easy to work with; is natural, not synthetic. Also, because this product will be advertised in the United States, there will be a great demand for Chinese silk by Americans and therefore good profits to be made.

2. <u>Apparel manufacturers.</u> For this second target group the message is essentially the same as the message to designers, although we might want to stress the potential profitability of silk even more.

3. <u>Retailers.</u> To this group we want to convey the idea that Chinese silk appeals especially to the purchasers of high-quality products; that customers will respond to the advertising for Chinese silk.

4. <u>Consumers,</u> Specifically ACHIEVERS and the SOCIETALLY CONSCIOUS. We want to persuade this fourth and final target that Chinese silk looks good; is of the highest quality; is unique and prestigious; is natural, not synthetic.

And with all of these groups, we need to differentiate Chinese silk from other silk.

As agreed, you'll want three weeks for a "first pass," and then I'll meet you and your group in Los Angeles to make sure we're in agreement on the direction you've developed.

See you April 20.

6. *Behavior*
   Finally, a successful campaign will enhance the audience's attitudes toward a company or brand in a positive way—for example, they will purchase a product or switch brands.

IMPLEMENTING THE CREATIVE OBJECTIVES

In implementing these objectives, certain strategies are pursued. These strategies are difficult to codify because they are usually accomplished almost intuitively.

After understanding the target thoroughly, the next step is to select the *crucial attribute* (sometimes referred to as the *unique selling proposition*); that is, the quality that makes our brand unique. It requires us to differentiate ourselves from competitive brands, to stake out a position for our brand that appeals to our target group. This position is preferably one that is unoccupied by competitive brands. If no such unoccupied position exists, we are forced to compete head-to-head with our rivals—that is, to compete with other brands on their grounds.

The next aspect of the creative strategy is to select the proper tone for the advertising, one that is in keeping with our audience, our message, and the media in which the advertising will appear. To advertise a diamond ring with a tonality that is romantic and emotional is certainly appropriate. To advertise industrial diamonds that way would not be. To advertise either in publications like *Casket and Sunnyside* or the *Angus Journal*, regardless of how economical those magazines might be, would make no sense at all.

The final aspect of the creative strategy is to convey images that are relevant to our product, our market positioning, and our audience. This step is accomplished through language, graphics, music, and casting.

THE CREATIVE WORK FOR THE CHINESE SILK CAMPAIGN

Doing an image campaign for China proved to be a fascinating challenge: to communicate the reality of China and its products within the context of what Americans understand about China. As the research showed, Americans' attitudes and conceptions of China are likely to be very different from those the Chinese feel about themselves and their country.

As an example, if we were to create an image campaign for China that would actually run in China, our efforts would probably focus on China's greatest resource and treasure: its people. Our goal, however, was to create a China campaign for Americans. Accordingly, the Chinese who viewed the campaign saw many things that may have surprised them but were actually quite appropriate for communicating to American audiences. We took much of our strategic direction from our research. Our creative strategy was geared toward what Americans saw as China's strengths. Therefore, much of our campaign is tied into the strengths of the ancient arts and "Old World" craftsmanship.

Our first step was to design a logo that could be used for Chinese silk and other products made in China. We opted for a simple Chinese character in our logo design, a character that stands for "treasures." We chose to go with an older version of the character (Figure 6-1), even though we knew that in China a more modern ideogram is commonly used. We made that choice because we were addressing an American audience to whom the more contemporary ideogram (Figure 6-2) looked as much Arabic as Chinese.

The advertising we developed is different in tone from that which the Chinese are used to seeing. We followed the American cultural preference for

Chap. 6 / The Creative Work 67

宝

Figure 6-1 Old Chinese Character for "Treasures."

宝

Figure 6-2 Modern Chinese Character for "Treasures."

provocative, exciting, and dramatic advertising rather than the more tranquil Chinese variety.

An old Chinese proverb states: "Seeing once is better than hearing a hundred times." This, then, would be the appropriate place to look at the campaign developed as an image campaign for China and the campaign to sell Chinese silk.

The ads and storyboards on the following pages were developed as

- an image campaign for China,
- a consumer campaign for Chinese silk, and
- a garment industry trade campaign for Chinese silk.

IMAGE CAMPAIGN

Figure 6-3 The logo for the Chinese image campaign.

Figure 6-4 The first in a series of mockups for three magazine ads featuring traditional Chinese products. This one sells the virtues of Chinese jade. Note: in these three ads, the body copy is not actual. It consists of random letters in paragraph form to indicate the design of the advertisement. (Photograph courtesy of Jade N Gem Corporation, Los Angeles.)

Chap. 6 / The Creative Work

Figure 6-5 This ad sells the beauty and quality of Chinese rugs. (Photograph courtesy of Charles I. Rostov.)

Figure 6-6 The third ad in the series describes the glories of Chinese silk. (Photograph courtesy of Royal Silk Co.)

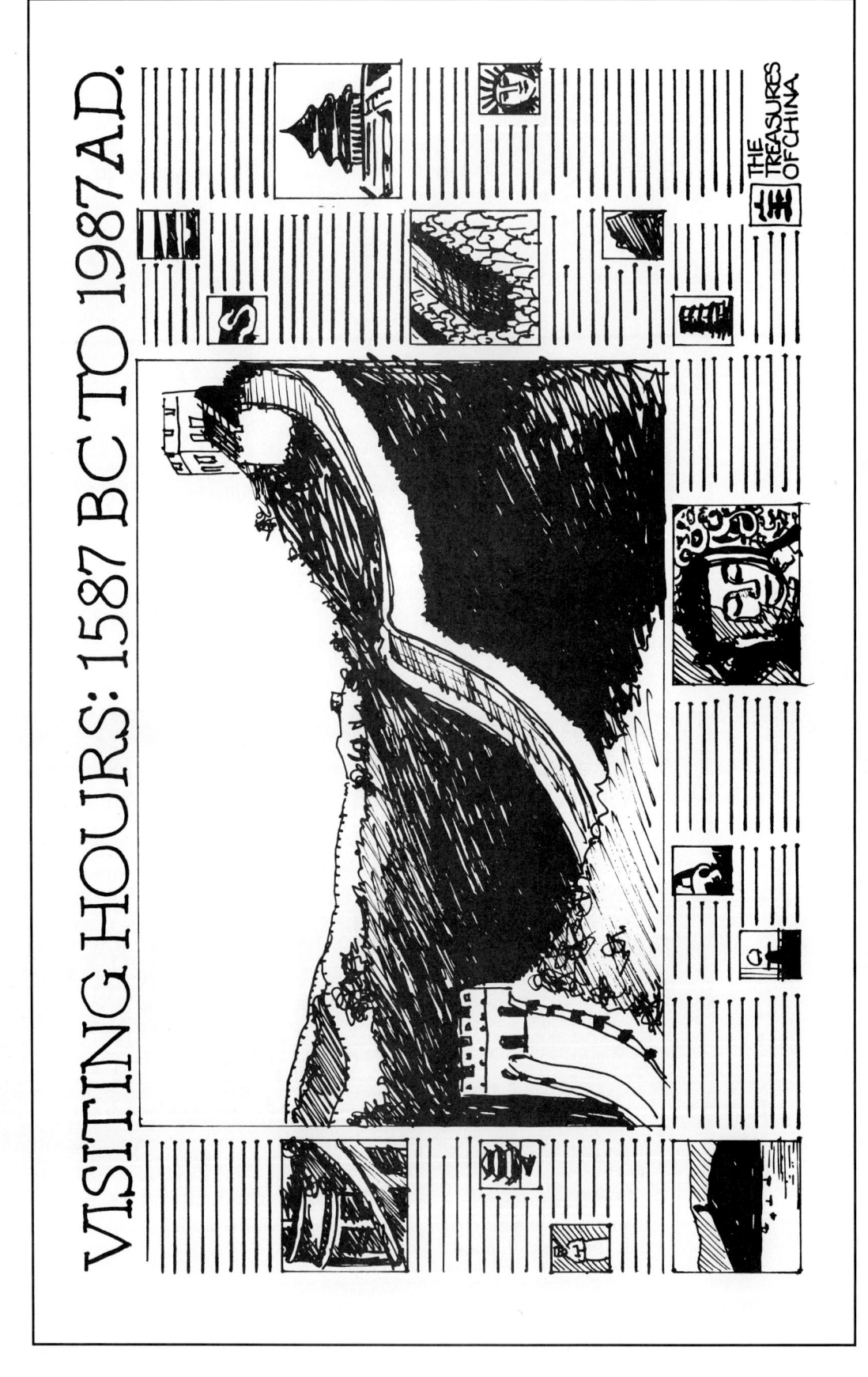

Figure 6-7 Artist's rendering of an ad in a second series in the Chinese image campaign.

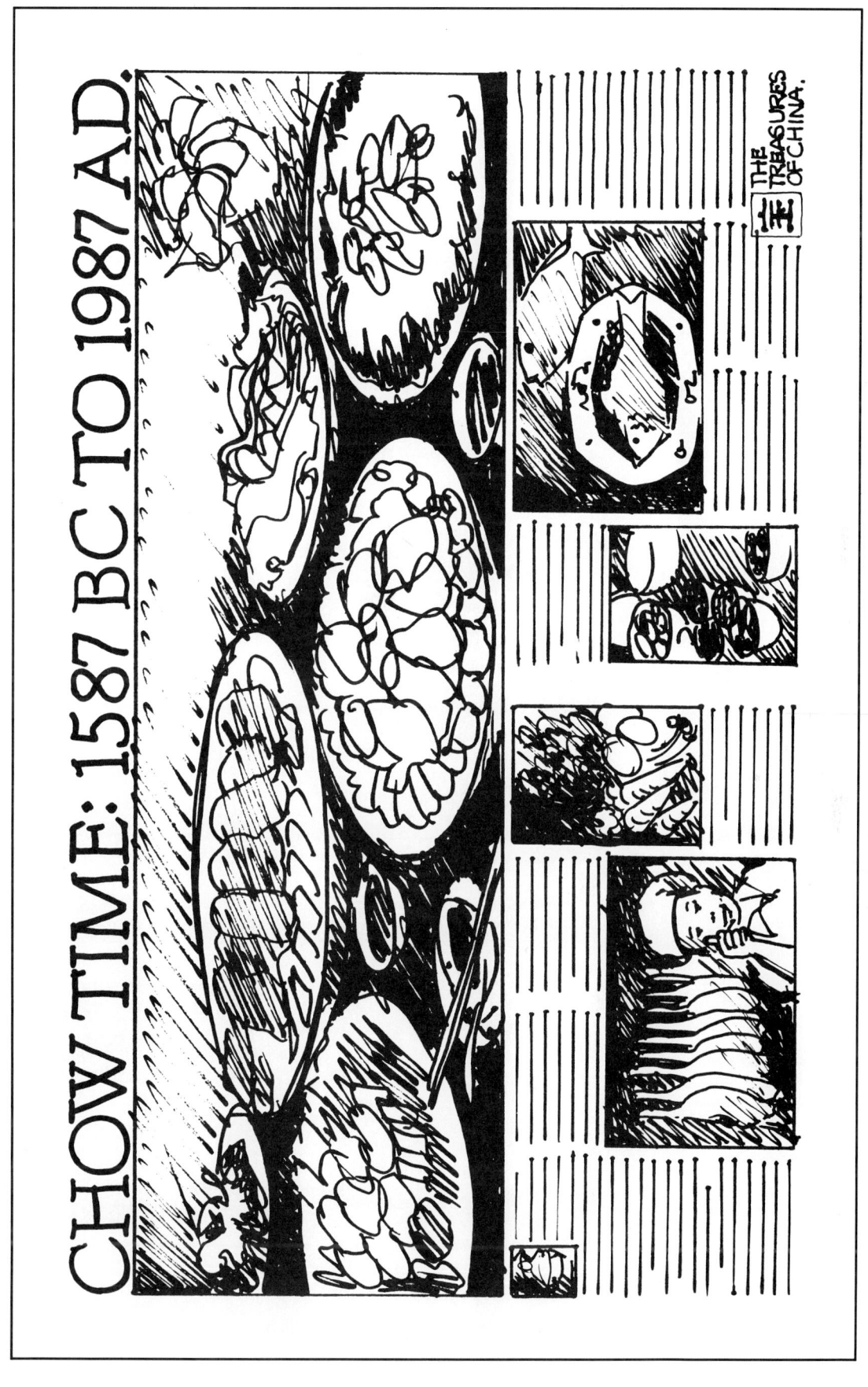

Figure 6-8 Artist's rendering of a magazine ad in the Chinese image campaign.

THE TREASURES OF CHINA
"SILK/NATIONAL TREASURE"   :30

CP 7303

(MUSIC UNDER)
ANNCR: (VO) The artistry of China lives

through an ancestry of exquisite craftsmanship

born from generation to generation.

From artist to artist,

this timeless succession of cultural celebration

is unequaled in history.

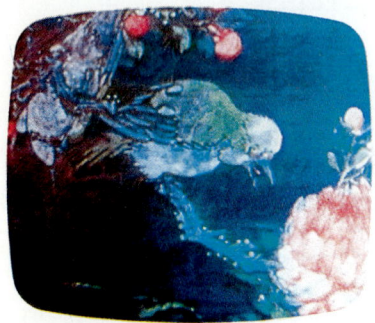

It is a tradition that speaks pride.

That breathes honor.

And that remains unbroken

even after 5000 years.

The treasures of China.

The Treasures of China.

Bozell, Jacobs, Kenyon & Eckhardt

Figure 6-9 Storyboard for television commercial—silk as a Chinese national treasure.

72

Chap. 6 / The Creative Work   73

Figure 6-10 The proposed logo for Chinese silk.

Figure 6-11 The first of three mockups of consumer-magazine ads on Chinese silk. (Photograph courtesy of Bonnie Boerer and Company.)

Figure 6-12 The second ad in the Chinese silk consumer campaign. Photograph courtesy of Carolee Designs, Inc., 385 5th Avenue, New York, NY 10016

Figure 6-13 The third ad completing the consumer print series. (Photograph courtesy of Corneliani U.S.A., Inc.)

Figure 6-14 Layout of an ad to the trade featuring an unexpected "Italian fashion expert."

Figure 6-15 An exceptional "Chinese translator"—Ralph Lauren.

Figure 6-16 Another unexpected twist, this time a different kind of French fashion designer.

Figure 6-17 The first in a series of three provocative layouts aimed at the trade.

Figure 6-18 Two more ads in the series targeted to the garment industry.

79

THE SILK OF CHINA
"SILK DRESS"   :30

CP 7301

(SIMPLE, EXOTIC CHINESE FLUTE & PERCUSSION MUSIC)

ANNCR: (VO) China.

Timeless in its history.

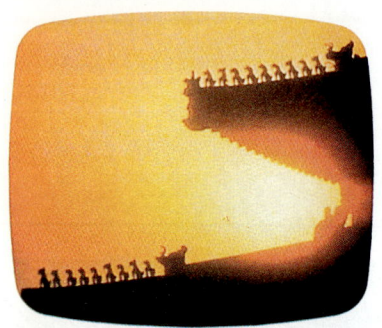

Peerless in its cultural achievements.

China's vast treasures...

have been coveted by man for centuries.

But none more than this

mystical cocoon. For this is the source of pure Chinese silk.

(MUSIC SEGUES INTO CONTEMPORARY JAZZ FLUTE & PERCUSSION) Shimmering, sensuous, seductive silk.

The living, breathing, 5000 year old legend.

The silk of China.

The Silk of China.

Bozell, Jacobs, Kenyon & Eckhardt

Figure 6-19 Storyboard of a 30-second television commercial on Chinese silk.

80

THE SILK OF CHINA
"SILK SUIT"   :30

CP 7302

(MUSIC UNDER)
ANNCR: (VO) The immeasurable legacy of China

endures in its architecture.

Grandly withstanding

the ravages of time.

But China's noblest structure

was not crafted by man.

For this is the cocoon of a silkworm.

The architect of pure Chinese silk.

Lustrous, luxurious, luscious silk.

The living, breathing, 5000 year old legend.

The silk of China.

The Silk of China.

Bozell, Jacobs, Kenyon & Eckhardt

Figure 6-20 Storyboard of a second television commercial selling Chinese silk.

Memorandum

Bozell, Jacobs, Kenyon & Eckhardt, Inc.
Advertising

MEMO TO: John LaPick

FROM: Jaye S. Niefeld

RE: Beijing Creative Work

The rough TV commercials and print ads look just great! If you execute them as beautifully as the concepts, we'll have an absolutely smashing presentation. The "Treasures of China" logo your people developed is also exactly what I wanted.

Please hold off on final executions for the ads and commercials until Joe Wang and Joseph Tong have seen the roughs -- just to make sure we haven't violated some cultural taboos that our audience simply could not stand. This review will take less than a week, and I'll get back to you immediately after that.

Please express my appreciation to all of the people in your department who have worked on the project.

Cordially,

Memorandum

Bozell. Jacobs. Kenyon & Eckhardt, Inc.
Advertising

MEMO TO: Jaye Niefeld
           John LaPick

FROM: Terry Gruggen

RE: People's Republic of China, Hong Kong Meeting

The purpose of this memorandum is to recap my meeting in Hong Kong with Michael Anderson, Joseph Wang (both of BJK&E), and Joseph Tong (General Manager of China-Link). The meeting was held to flush out any cultural snafus in our creative direction, and to address details pertinent to the presentation in June. The following summarizes our meeting:

THEMELINE ("Treasures of China")

    A. The Chinese characters used in our themeline (i.e., on the cover of the leave-behind piece) are old (i.e., outdated) Chinese characters. We should make certain that the characters are the modern version.

    B. Joseph Wang strongly encouraged us to extend the themeline to a variety of Chinese treasures. As an example:

        - The Treasures of China: Silk
        - The Treasures of China: Jade
        - The Treasures of China: Cuisine

    Accordingly, the image campaign could be executed against a number of various "treasures" ... for extension beyond what we currently have. He also encouraged us to consider executing the themeline on the leave-behind piece in the aforementioned manner (i.e., "The Treasures of China: Silk).

Page Two

CREATIVE EXECUTIONS

    A. Overall

- Both Joseph Wang and Joseph Tong felt quite strongly that our "treasures" campaign was too arts and handicrafts oriented ... and that these would be perceived by the Chinese as being part of their "ancient" history. While it is certainly appropriate to include them as part of the image campaign, we should also include "treasures" that the Chinese perceive as treasures of modern China. These would include such treasures as **tourism**, Chinese cuisine, medicine (herb and tonic orientation) and the **people of China**. They felt the latter would be a real "hot button" with the audience in Beijing, for the Chinese consider their people a tremendous resource and therefore, treasure.

    B. Television

- In reviewing the television with them, they both made a comment on using the sun as a device throughout the spot. They associate the sun with Japan rather than China (land of the rising sun).

- Similarly, the frame with the peasant walking on the beach conjured up images of Japan. <u>They suggested that a Chinese person walking through a mulberry field would be more appropriate.</u>

- They advised us to make sure that any architecture portrayed is Chinese, not Japanese. The architecture rendered in the storyboard is Chinese.

- The Chinese are literal, and therefore we should not take license with the colors of the cocoons. They noted that there is no such thing as pink cocoons.

Page Three

    C. Music

        - This is their opinion on the cuts from the cassette you provided me:

CUT	TITLE	APPROPRIATE
#1	Angel's Flight	Yes
#2	VAJRA	No
#3	Wheel of Dreams	Yes
#4	Move the Clouds	No
#5	A Thousand Teardrops	Yes
#6	Ariki	No

    D. Print Advertising

- **Ad with Jade Bowl**
  Headline: Jade/Carpets/Porcelain/Silk/Sculpture.
- Generally no problem with the ad.
- Again, all of the treasures pertain to ancient China. Consider utilizing treasures of modern China (as mentioned earlier).

- **Ad of Woman on Beach**
  Headline: The most sensuous thing in Italian pants is Chinese silks.
- Culturally, it is important that we avoid visuals that are provocative and/or sexually suggestive. They felt that this ad could be fixed by simply closing a couple more buttons on her blouse.

- **Ad of Woman's Torso in Silk Blouse**
  Headline: The legend of the hand-fed blouse.
- No problem here other than too much exposed breast ... nothing that a few buttons won't cure.

- **Ad of Old Chinese Man**
  Headline: Italian fashion expert.
- They almost fell out of their chairs at this one. They soon came around but only after considerable discussion about how we must set up our creative presentation (more about this later). They had a problem because this man is not how the Chinese would portray a silk worker. Anyway, the ad lives as is.

Page Four

OVERALL PRESENTATION

    A. Creative
- Joseph Wang and Joseph Tong could not stress enough the importance of setting up the creative portion of the presentation. It must be made **very clear** to the audience in Beijing that there are dramatic cultural differences between advertising in China versus advertising in the U.S. We must communicate that the ads we will be showing are designed for our culture (e.g., "advertising in the West must appeal to the West"). They both emphasized that the setup for our creative presentation must be explained in depth, and that the ads we are about to show them are indeed "sophisticated to a Western audience." If this step is not done properly, they feel that we'll lose our audience ... especially with ads like "ITALIAN FASHION EXPERT." The Chinese will not be able to grasp the subtleties of the contradiction.

- Another point they mentioned is that all Chinese advertising contains some sort of response mechanism (usually a phone number). They thought the Chinese in the audience may have a difficult time relating to ads without a response mechanism. This is quite obviously a creative call, and I only mention it because they did.

    B. Media

- Both Wang and Tong felt it would be inappropriate to tie ourselves to a firm budget number for the presentation. They stated that, culturally, the Chinese are accustomed to considerable flexibility in their working relationships. Accordingly, they suggested that we present a <u>number</u> of alternatives (maximum to minimum) relative to media budget: a full-blown plan would cost $10,000,000; here is what you can do for $5,000,000 and $1,000,000; and here's what a $300,000 plan would look like. The Chinese prefer to work with multiple alternatives, and they felt this kind of approach would play quite well with the audience.

They emphasized quite strongly that the media presentation must be "macro" in nature. If we get into detail, we'll lose our audience.

Page Five

LEAVE-BEHIND PIECE

- Joseph Wang is currently estimating the cost of producing the leave-behind piece in Hong Kong. I left the piece with them so that they have the precise measurements and distance between the rings. They are costing out the following:

    - Vinyl notebooks, wrapped in silk ribbon with IAMC and BJK&E logo on front.
    - Silk notebook, wrapped in silk ribbon, with IAMC
    - and BJK&E logo on front.
    - Possibility of sealing ribbon with wax seal.

- The felt they might be able to get a good price on reproducing 4/C storyboards.

- We need to clear Chinese Customs with our leave-behind piece, but they did not feel this would be any problem.

Both Joseph Wang and Joseph Tong were extremely helpful in providing input for this presentation. They both offered to review all creative, presentation materials and presentation scripts for cultural snafus. In fact, they strongly encouraged us to do so to avoid any embarassment at the presentation in Beijing. Judging by the quality of the comments I received from them, I would emphatically recommend that we do so.

If you have any questions or comments, please don't hesitate to contact me.

Thank you.

cc: Murray Smith (New York)
Michael Anderson (Hong Kong)
Joseph Wang (Hong Kong)
Joseph Tong (China-Link)

CREATIVE RESEARCH

Because American consumers are exposed to over $100 billion worth of advertising each year, it is important for individual advertisers to know that their advertising breaks through the clutter and communicates the proper messages. Accordingly, advertisers frequently conduct research to ensure that their communications strategies are clearly conveyed by their ads and commercials. We, too, decided to measure the impact of our advertising for China and Chinese silk.

The specific objective of the research was to evaluate the effect of our two advertising campaigns on the consumer's desire to buy products from China. We asked specific questions to elicit information in three areas:

1. To what extent does exposure to advertising increase people's willingness to consider purchasing products from China?
2. How believable are the advertisements?
3. What key elements are communicated to the consumer through specific ads and/or commercials? What impressions are created?

The study was conducted by means of interviews with consumers in shopping malls in both Los Angeles and Chicago. Two hundred interviews were completed. The interviews were divided evenly between men and women. To qualify, respondents had to have a household income of at least $25,000.

The results showed that 75 percent of those surveyed came away from the interview with the idea that Chinese products represented quality and craftsmanship. Table 6-1 shows how those surveyed viewed three factors.

TABLE 6-1

CONTENT OF THE COMMUNICATION	POSITIVE VIEW OF CHINA
Chinese products, quality, craftsmanship	75%
Vases, porcelain	32
Chinese history, culture, art	28

Our survey also found that the ads increased people's interest in buying products from China. Significantly, the ads featuring clothing and silk seemed to be the most powerful in that respect.

EXPOSURE TO THE ADS

Table 6-2 shows that total interest in buying the products featured in the advertising increased after exposure to individual ads. We were of course pleased that the ads had such a positive impact.

TABLE 6-2

ADVERTISEMENT	TOTAL INTEREST IN BUYING PRODUCTS AFTER AD EXPOSURE (IN PERCENT)
"Legend of the Hand-Fed Blouse"	77
"The Most Sensuous Thing"	67
"The Treasures of China"	63

Chap. 6 / The Creative Work   89

BELIEVABILITY OF THE ADS

When we asked people about the believability of the advertising, approximately 90 percent responded that they found the ads totally believable.

INTEREST IN BUYING PRODUCTS OF CHINA

Interest Score 77%

Interest Score 67%

Interest Score 63%

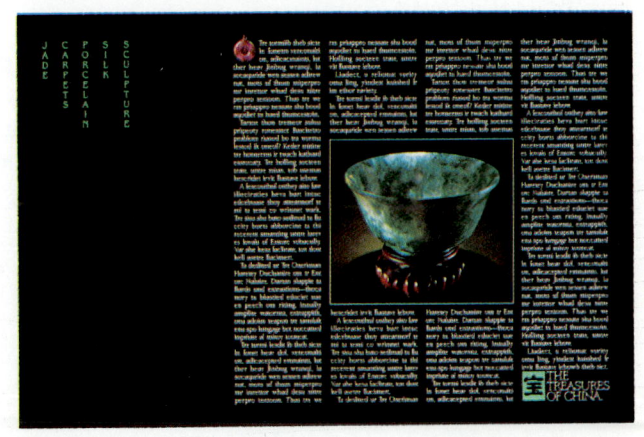

ADVERTISING COMMUNICATION

The last thing we measured in our creative research was advertising communication. Our survey indicated that the two ads featuring silk clothing communicated strongly the quality and craftsmanship of Chinese silk (Table 6-3).

TABLE 6-3

ADVERTISEMENT	PERCENT WHO MENTIONED THE QUALITY AND CRAFTSMANSHIP OF CHINESE SILK
"The Legend of the Hand-Fed Blouse"	79
"The Most Sensuous Thing"	65

OVERALL RESULTS

Overall, we were impressed with the very positive results of the creative research. As a result of these findings, we were confident that the Chinese silk campaign could effectively break through the clutter created by the billions of dollars worth of advertising targeted at the American public each year.

Chapter 7

Merchandising

Merchandising has been defined as "the activities of manufacturers and middlemen which are designed to adjust the merchandise produced or offered for sale to customer demand." This classic definition has probably been overtaken by actual in-market practices. In current parlance merchandising is usually defined as "the efforts of manufacturers and middlemen (in this case designers, manufacturers, and retailers) to stimulate consumer demand through product displays, sales promotion, and the like."

Figure 7-1 The entrance to the Neiman Marcus elevator bank. Notice "The Treasures of China" logo incorporated in the carpet. (Courtesy of Neiman Marcus. Photograph: Donald F. Wristen, D.F.W. Photography, Inc.)

Memorandum

Bozell, Jacobs, Kenyon & Eckhardt, Inc.
Advertising

MEMO TO: Les Gibson

FROM: Jaye S. Niefeld

RE: China Silk Leave-Behind Piece and Merchandising Section

I can't tell you, Les, how delighted I am to have you take over the responsibility for producing the leave-behind piece and for developing the Merchandising section of the presentation. My thoughts on the two are these:

1. <u>Leave-behind piece</u>.

    - A three-ring binder, covered in silk if it's affordable, in a silklike synthetic if not.

    - The contents should be the verbatim speeches of the presenters. Each speaker's part should be a separate section, with his picture and title at the front of each section.

    - All of the creative work should be reproduced in four-color, if affordable.

    - We'll need 2,000 copies, of which 1,500 should be sent to Beijing (Great Hall of the People). The balance should be sent to the New York office for use by the International Division.

    - Make free use of our "Treasures of China" logo throughout. I'm enclosing the copy and graphics for the binder cover.

2. The Merchandising section.

As you know, we're operating on the assumption that the China-image campaign and the Chinese-silk advertising will have little money available for conventional media. Therefore, a strong public relations program and a strong merchandising program will have to be the major factors in publicizing Chinese silk.

It will be difficult to explain to our audience of mostly Third World representatives the concept of merchandising without giving them a specific example. What I'd like to do is "rent" a department store overnight and during the night put up the signs and other displays which demonstrate what a storewide promotion on Chinese silk would look like.

Apart from signs of the "Treasures of China" logo, we should show what displays of silk dresses and accessories, silk draperies, silk suits, and silk rugs would look like.

I'm sure you grasp what I'm trying to achieve and are probably far ahead of me. I know it will be tough to get everything in place and photographed in one night, but I hope it can be done.

Please let me know soonest whether what I've suggested is feasible and if not, what else we can do to achieve the same effect.

Cordially,

Les Gibson was the manager of the agency's special accounts group.

We recognized at the outset of this project that the Chinese probably would not have a budget large enough to fund strong media campaigns for China and Chinese silk. As mentioned earlier, we felt that we would have to rely on merchandising and public relations to flesh out the advertising.

It was our goal to have the prestigious department stores in the United States purchase a wide variety of Chinese silk products, display them with flair, and then advertise these storewide promotions heavily.

Figure 7-2 Counter card on the display case featuring Chinese jewelry. (Courtesy of Neiman Marcus. Photograph: Donald F. Wristen, D.F.W. Photography, Inc.)

Figure 7-3 Exhibit featuring a Chinese dragon joust. (Courtesy of Neiman Marcus. Photograph: Donald F. Wristen, D.F.W. Photography, Inc.)

Memorandum

Bozell, Jacobs, Kenyon & Eckhardt, Inc.
Advertising

MEMO TO: Jaye S. Niefeld

FROM: Les Gibson

RE: Beijing Project

First, the bad news. Your proposed budget for the 2,000 leave-behind books -- including 20 pages of four-color work -- just won't be enough. I'll have to increase the dollar amount by 50%. Sorry, but there really is nothing that we can do to cut that figure, particularly in light of the tight deadlines.

Now for the good news. You wanted to show how we could merchandise the Chinese silk advertising campaign by demonstrating how a department store might create a storewide Chinese silk promotion -- in their dress department, the menswear department, and their furnishings and accessories departments.

Well, we ran into some luck. I talked with the manager of the Neiman-Marcus store in Dallas about working something out with him. He said the store had actually had a "Products of China" promotion a few years ago, and he had lots of color photographs of the various departments' displays.

I feel we can use several of these photographs and "strip-in" our Chinese silk logo in the appropriate places, rather than trying to set up our own original displays. In other words, we can accomplish what you want in the photo retouching lab, rather than in the department store.

The result is a lot less hassle and faster turnaround time, and we can save almost as much money as we'll have to overspend on the leave-behinds. Hope you like the way we Texans perform.

Best wishes,

Les Gibson

Figure 7-4 The Neiman Marcus "Pacific Trading Company" with ceiling banners proclaiming that "The Treasures of China" are to be found here. (Courtesy of Neiman Marcus. Photograph: Donald F. Wristen, D.F.W. Photography, Inc.)

Figure 7-5 A wine display features "The Treasures of China." (Courtesy of Neiman Marcus. Photograph: Donald F. Wristen, D.F.W. Photography, Inc.)

Chap. 7 / Merchandising

Figure 7-6 Chinese artifacts are some of the many Chinese products offered at Neiman Marcus. (Courtesy of Neiman Marcus. Photograph: Donald F. Wristen, D.F.W. Photography, Inc.)

Figure 7-7 Accessories made in China are also flagged. (Courtesy of Neiman Marcus. Photograph: Donald F. Wristen, D.F.W. Photography, Inc.)

Figure 7-8 Imaginative background sets are created on the retail floor to attract customers to "The Silk of China." (Courtesy of Neiman Marcus. Photograph: Donald F. Wristen, D.F.W. Photography, Inc.)

Figure 7-9 Signs point to the diversified and historical uses of Chinese silk. (Courtesy of Neiman Marcus. Photograph: Donald F. Wristen, D.F.W. Photography, Inc.)

Chap. 7 / Merchandising

Figure 7-10 The Chinese silk logo is to be found throughout the store in the form of signs and hang tags. (Courtesy of Neiman Marcus. Photograph: Donald F. Wristen, D.F.W. Photography, Inc.)

Memorandum

Bozell, Jacobs, Kenyon & Eckhardt, Inc.
Advertising

MEMO TO: Murray L. Smith

FROM: Jaye S. Niefeld

RE: Clearances

I've written a statement about Chinese silk which I'd like attributed to Ralph Lauren -- provided, of course, that he agrees with it. Since you know him personally, I'd appreciate it if you would get a release from him for the statement.

If there is something he disagrees with, see if you can come up with a favorable comment that more closely incorporates his views.

The statement is this:

"I try to understand the various customers I design for. What will make each person feel better about herself or himself? What are the lifestyle trends that will have an impact on the way the customer lives, and how will clothes fit into those lifestyle trends?

"And then, I want to offer things that are unusual and which have class. Things that are aesthetically pleasing.

"Interestingly, Chinese silk can be all of those things -- unusual, classy and aesthetically pleasing. And if various segments of the American public are shown designs that fit into their lifestyles, the potential for Chinese silk can be very great."

Murray, I appreciate your help.

Cordially,

Chapter 8

Conclusion

CONCLUDING SPEECH DELIVERED TO THE BEIJING CONFERENCE

Our assignment today was to demonstrate how an image campaign for China would have a beneficial effect on the sale of Chinese products. I hope we have fulfilled that assignment—and we thank you for sharing the vision of what our "Treasures of China" campaign could accomplish for the sale of Chinese products such as silk.

We believe that this campaign can create a substantially greater demand in the United States for Chinese silk—at highly profitable prices.

What we want to convey to the West is the message that the famous designer, Oscar de la Renta, first stated, "Silk does for the body what diamonds do for the hand."

It was a privilege to present to you our thoughts and ideas, as it was exciting to participate in this Third World Advertising Congress. You have been a most gracious audience.

BJK&E STEALS THE SHOW

More than a few eyebrows were raised at BJK&E's presentation at the recent Third World Advertising Congress in China, Alan Dunachie reports.

It may not have been the best session of the *Third World Advertising Congress* last month in Beijing, but Bozell, Jacobs, Kenyon & Eckhardt's public pitch for Chinese business was certainly the showiest, the most expensive, and, for days, *the* talking point of delegates. Moreover, not only did it manage to encapsulate many of the issues the Congress was held to address, but it also demonstrated what an event like this can achieve and, alternately, where it will always fail.

There was nothing coy about BJK&E's centrepiece presentation. The agency's lineup of top executives went for the jugular: China needed to market and advertise itself and its products abroad, they said, and here were the campaigns to do it—an image push on the one hand and a campaign for Chinese silk on the other. Both were aimed at U.S. audiences.

They showed TV and print ads, talked the audience through pre-test research and, understanding that the PRC's foreign exchange reserves are ex-

Memorandum

Bozell. Jacobs. Kenyon & Eckhardt. Inc.
Advertising

MEMO TO: John La Pick   CC: Charles D. Peebler, Jr
           Les Gibson   Murray L. Smith
           Ward White   David A. Bell
           Renee Fraser
           James Spero
           Terry Gruggen
           Diane Bonner

FROM: Jaye Niefeld

RE: Beijing Presentation

It's over, and it was a smash! Sorry all of you weren't there to get the audience reaction directly, but the enclosed article from INTERNATIONAL MEDIA gives you some of the flavor of the event.

Thanks again. You should all be proud of your contributions to what turned out to be a unique and class presentation.

Cordially,

tremely limited, proposed that all China would have to put up would be U.S. $350,000. The rest—between $2 million and $3 million—could probably be squeezed out of U.S. retailers.

What shook BJK&E's fellow travellers to China, in particular those few agencies that have invested heavily for years in their Chinese operations for little profit, was BJK&E's audacity. Here was an agency that had no presence in the PRC, an agency that unlike its rivals had not followed the established and necessary path of throwing money down the PRC's bottomless pit to establish its creditability (apart, that is, from the $150,000 or so BJK&E was rumoured to have spent on the presentation) and had no real intention of doing so. The agency was not even in the top five of Asia's agency networks. Yet BJK&E stole the show.

Source: *International Media*, July 1987.

Bottomless Pit

To make matters worse, the credentials presentations—for that is what they all were—by [the other agencies] the next day suffered by comparison to BJK&E's slick effort. The moral was very clear. If you *are* going to do a straight pitch for business, at least entertain your audience when you do it. [The other agencies] were supposed to give their audience some insight into "setting up an agency in China." What they actually gave was: "We've set up our agency in China and here are some of our ads."

So they have no ground to cavil about the heavy sell of BJK&E's presentation. . . . Of the many pitches made during the week of the Congress, at least BJK&E's was the most original. . . .